Classroom Management

A Survival Guide

Deslea Konza
Jessica Grainger
Keith Bradshaw

CENGAGE
Learning™

Australia • Brazil • Japan • Korea • Mexico • Singapore • Spain • United Kingdom • United States

CENGAGE Learning

Classroom Management: A Survival Guide
1st Edition
Deslea Konza
Jessica Grainger
Keith Bradshaw

Production controller: Tanya Simmons
Reprint: Magda Koralewska

Any URLs contained in this publication were checked for currency during the production process. Note, however, that the publisher cannot vouch for the ongoing currency of URLs.

First published in 2001 by Social Science Press
Reprinted in 2006 by Cengage Learning Australia

© 2001 Deslea Konza, Jessica Grainger and Keith Bradshaw

Copyright Notice
This Work is copyright. No part of this Work may be reproduced, stored in a retrieval system, or transmitted in any form or by any means without prior written permission of the Publisher. Except as permitted under the *Copyright Act 1968*, for example any fair dealing for the purposes of private study, research, criticism or review, subject to certain limitations. These limitations include: Restricting the copying to a maximum of one chapter or 10% of this book, whichever is greater; providing an appropriate notice and warning with the copies of the Work disseminated; taking all reasonable steps to limit access to these copies to people authorised to receive these copies; ensuring you hold the appropriate Licences issued by the Copyright Agency Limited ("CAL"), supply a remuneration notice to CAL and pay any required fees. For details of CAL licences and remuneration notices please contact CAL at Level 15, 233 Castlereagh Street, Sydney NSW 2000, Tel: (02) 9394 7600, Fax: (02) 9394 7601
Email: info@copyright.com.au
Website: www.copyright.com.au

For product information and technology assistance,
in Australia call **1300 790 853**;
in New Zealand call **0800 449 725**

For permission to use material from this text or product, please email
aust.permissions@cengage.com

ISBN 978 0 17 013415 6

Cengage Learning Australia
Level 7, 80 Dorcas Street
South Melbourne, Victoria Australia 3205

Cengage Learning New Zealand
Unit 4B Rosedale Office Park
331 Rosedale Road, Albany, North Shore 0632, NZ

For learning solutions, visit **cengage.com.au**

Printed in Australia by Ligare Pty Ltd.
6 7 8 9 10 11 12 16 15 14 13 12

Contents

AUTHORS' NOTE vi
FOREWORD vii

PART ONE   **A Navigation Guide** 1

CHAPTER ONE   UNDERSTANDING INDIVIDUAL DIFFERENCES AND THEIR
                            EFFECT ON BEHAVIOUR 2
    Introduction 2
    Age 2
    Gender Differences 5
    Physical and Sensory Abilities 5
    Cultural Background 6
    Social Background 7
    Temperament and Personality 7
    Cognitive Styles and Abilities 9
    Asperger's Syndrome 10
    Attention Deficit Hyperactivity Disorder (ADHD) 13
    Oppositional Defiant Disorder (ODD) 19
    Conduct Disorder (CD) 22

CHAPTER TWO   CREATING A POSITIVE LEARNING ENVIRONMENT 24
    Introduction 24
    The Physical Setting 24
    The Emotional Climate 28
    Strategies for Creating a Positive Emotional Climate 30
    Classroom Activities to Build Self Esteem and a Feeling of Belonging ... 35

PART TWO   **Setting Sail in Fair Weather** 41

CHAPTER THREE   DEVELOPING CLASSROOM RULES AND ROUTINES 42
    Introduction 42
    The Importance of a Set of Rules or Code of Conduct 42
    General Principles for Developing Classroom Rules 44
    The Importance of Establishing Routines 48
    Some Ideas to Help You Organise Your Routines 51
    The Casual Teachers' Survival Guide 54
    The Casual Teachers' Survival Pack 58

CHAPTER FOUR   MANAGING BEHAVIOUR THROUGH EFFECTIVE TEACHING: THEORY AND PRACTICE 61

Introduction 61
Time on Task and Academic Engaged Time 61
The Principles of Effective Teaching 63
Putting it into Practice 71
Additional Strategies for More Demanding Students 75

CHAPTER FIVE   EXISTING MODELS OF BEHAVIOUR MANAGEMENT 79

Introduction 79
Group Management Models 80
Lee and Marlene Canter's Assertive Discipline 80
Fritz Redl 82
Frederic Jones 83
Jacob Kounin 85
The Behaviourist Model 87
The Cognitive Behavioural Model 88
Psychological or Needs-based Communication Models 90
Alfred Adler's Individual Psychology 90
Dreikurs and the Goals of Classroom Misbehaviour 90
Dinkmeyer, McKay and Dinkmeyer's S.T.E.T. Program 91
Maurice Balson 94
William Glasser's Choice Theory 95
An Eclectic Model 98
Bill Rogers' Decisive Discipline 98

PART THREE   Facing Squalls and Heavy Swells 101

CHAPTER SIX   RESPONDING TO DIFFICULT BEHAVIOURS: CLASSROOM STRATEGIES 102

Introduction 102
Principles of Behaviour Correction 103
Reward Systems 107
Developing Incentive Systems 108
Understanding Reinforcers 108
Implementing Incentive Schemes 108
Suggestions for Class and Individual Reward Systems 111
First Line of In-Class Defence 113
Second Line of In-Class Defence 114
Final Line of In-Class Defence 116

PART FOUR — Surviving Storms at Sea 120

CHAPTER SEVEN RESPONDING TO MORE DIFFICULT BEHAVIOURS:
MOVING OUTSIDE THE CLASSROOM 121

Introduction 121
Strategies to Deal with More Disruptive Behaviour 122
Analyse the Problem Situation 123
Conduct a Private Talk 124
Set up a Private Cueing System 127
Use Timers to Monitor Behaviour 128
Set Up a Monitoring Program 128
Rehearse Target Behaviours 130
Shape Desired Behaviours Using Encouragement 130
Draw Up a Contract 132

CHAPTER EIGHT MANAGING YOUR OWN RESPONSES 135

Introduction 135
Stress 136
Reactions to Stress 137
Changing Your Automatic Thoughts 143
Learning to 'Dispute' Negative Thoughts 144
Positive Self-talk Requires Practice 148
Keeping a Challenges Diary 149

REFERENCES 151

Authors' note

We struggled with the problem of his/her, he/she, him/her for both teachers and students throughout this book. We are acutely aware of the impact of constantly referring to a student as he (although there is ample evidence that most major behaviour problems exist in boys) and to teachers as she (although most teachers are female) but referring constantly to both genders greatly reduced the fluency and readability of the book. Where possible, we address the reader directly, and use the plural for students. Where this was not appropriate, we have chosen to alternate gender references in alternate chapters, thus in odd-numbered chapters students are male and teachers female; in even-numbered chapters, the reverse applies.

Foreward

One of the most daunting aspects of teaching is behaviour management. This is particularly the case for new teachers. Disruptive behaviour in the classroom, from excessive talking and interrupting, to the more serious defiant and aggressive behaviour, is a major cause of stress and teacher burnout, and one of the most often-quoted reasons for teachers leaving their profession.

This books aims to provide both new and practising teachers with information that will aid an understanding of student behaviour, and strategies that will limit disruptive behaviour and increase effective teaching time. Throughout the book, we have used the framework of a sailor preparing for, and setting out on, a journey, hence the teacher/sailor figure who appears at various intervals. We believe that there are many similarities between the experiences of a sailor preparing for a long journey and a teacher preparing for a new class.

Successful sailing requires careful planning and preparation. Sailors must check the navigation guides, assess the weather, organise supplies and ensure that their ship is seaworthy. Sailors must maintain the morale of their crew, be skilled in the many different facets of their craft, keep the ship in good order, be alert for bad weather and keep accurate logs. Sailors hope for good conditions but prepare for the worst conditions. Sailors must learn from those who have gone before: who have charted the waters, tested the weather, trialled new methods and survived difficult conditions; but they must also be prepared to go into uncharted territory when required. Finally, sailors must look after themselves as well as their crew if they are to complete their journey successfully.

Teachers are a lot like sailors

We believe that teachers' lives have many parallels with the above experiences and expectations, and so we provide this "navigation guide through today's classrooms".

Part One begins the "navigation guide". It focuses on preparation and planning for teaching. In order to teach successfully, you need to have a good understanding of your students, of how different each individual in your class may be, and how individual their needs may be.

You need to read your "navigation guide"

Being aware of how to provide an effective physical and emotional environment for your students is also part of the preparation phase.

Part Two will assist you to "set sail". It details how to establish the essential rules and routines for an effective learning environment. It provides a summary of the effective teaching literature, which highlights teaching techniques and strategies which have been found to increase the academic engagement and on-task behaviour of students. When students are busily engaged in the business of learning, they are not wandering around aimlessly, being disruptive or affecting the learning of others. This section also discusses existing models of behaviour management so you may learn from "those who have sailed these waters before".

Sometimes teaching is smooth sailing

Part Three focuses on what to do when, despite all your planning and preparation, you encounter difficult conditions. How do you maintain your course during "heavy swells and sudden squalls"? How can you encourage and motivate students who appear to have no intrinsic desire to learn, who move off-task easily, and who lack organisational and self-management skills? Important principles of classroom management are outlined and supported by specific strategies that will help you redirect your students using positive and respectful techniques.

Sometimes you meet heavy swells

Part Four provides a guide for surviving "storms at sea" - strategies that may assist you when conditions become extremely difficult. How can you help students who are continually disruptive, who challenge your right to teach, and your students' right to learn? Effective classroom management requires, on occasions, out-of-class strategies to support classroom-based strategies for students whose behaviour is extremely challenging. Dealing with very difficult behaviours can be an exhausting, stressful business. This section also outlines some strategies that may assist you in maintaining your own physical and emotional health.

You'll also strike storms at sea

Despite this rather challenging account of the role of the teacher, we would like to emphasise the fact that teaching can be a very rewarding profession. We, the authors, have enjoyed many years of teaching students of all ages, and although we could recount numerous stories of frustration and challenge (and occasional panic!), our strongest memories are of joy, when struggling students make a breakthrough; of wonder at what some students will overcome to achieve; and of pride that we may have helped them in their achievements. Connecting with students who are difficult to teach can be the most joyful and wondrous of all. Teaching students how to manage their own behaviour and live productively with a range of people is a gift that will empower your students for the rest of their lives. We hope this book helps you do just that.

Deslea Konza
Jessica Grainger
Keith Bradshaw

For Bert, a true friend and a dedicated teacher

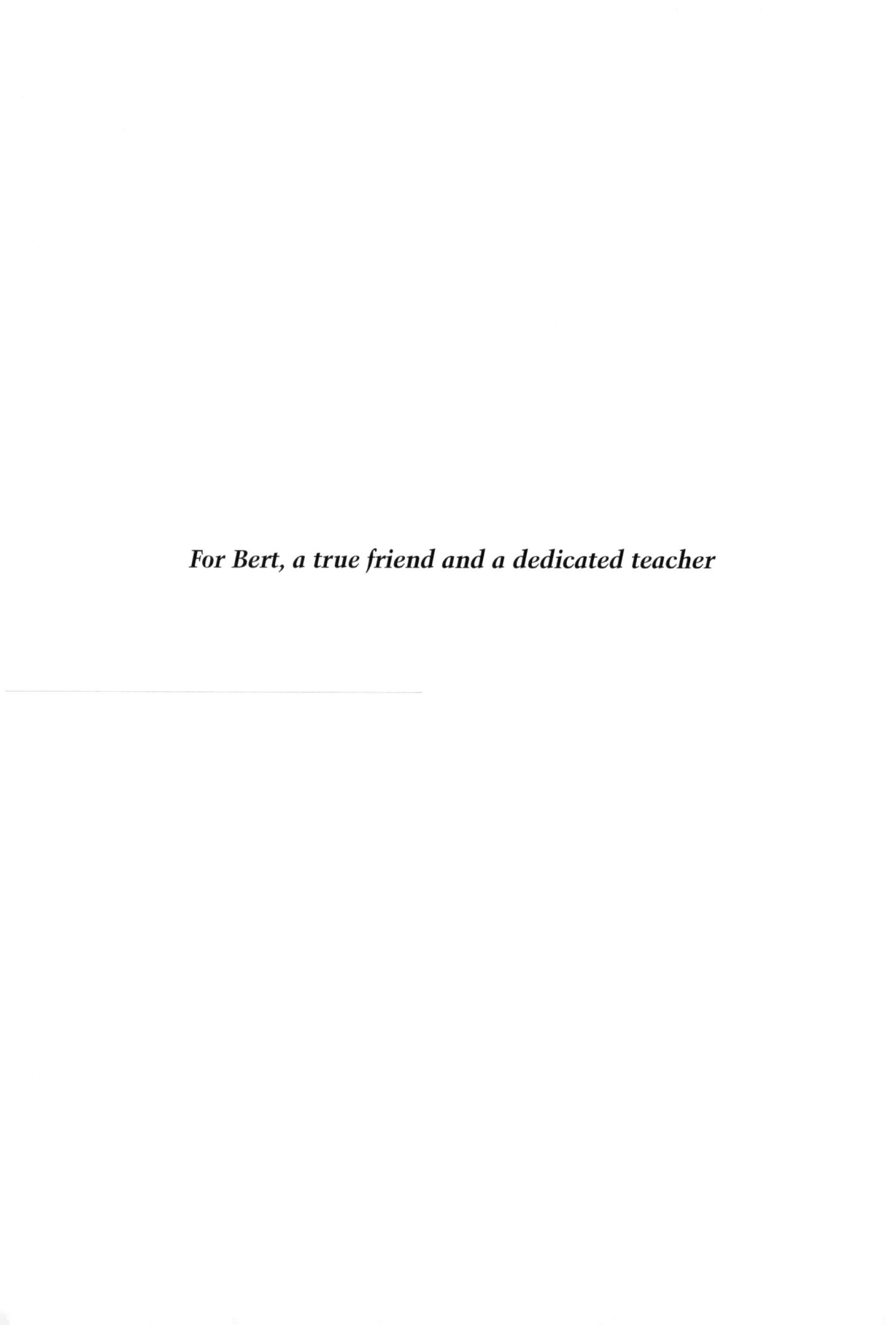

PART ONE

A NAVIGATION GUIDE

Chapter One

UNDERSTANDING INDIVIDUAL DIFFERENCES AND THEIR EFFECT ON BEHAVIOUR

Introduction

When you, as a teacher stand before a class, you are faced with a large number of *individuals*. Each of those individuals, even if aged only five years, will differ across a broad range of variables - cultural background, physical and cognitive ability, level of motivation, family support, and so on. In other words, each of those students has a separate physical, emotional and social history which will affect his attitude and inclinations towards learning and behaviour. It is a wise teacher who acknowledges these potential differences and makes an effort to understand where each student may be "coming from".

Consider the following ways in which students in a class may differ, and the impact these factors may have on their willingness to conform to the behaviour generally expected in a classroom. Consider also how these factors would affect the types of management strategies you need to use to nurture an effective learning environment.

Age

Clearly young children have different needs and will behave differently from older students. An understanding of what can be expected of students at different ages is important to ensure that your expectations are realistic and your management methods appropriate.

Most teachers are familiar with the stages of development authored by Piaget (1950; 1952; 1985). Based on these stages of cognitive development, Kohlberg (1969, 1976, 1978) developed a three-level, six-stage model of moral development. Kohlberg believed that people pass through defined stages in moral thinking from childhood to adulthood. These stages are dependent on achieving a certain cognitive level and on the development of inductive reasoning abilities. As individuals mature, they are able to take on additional perspectives other than their own. An understanding of these stages helps teachers select the correct strategy when trying to redirect behaviour. Table 1.1 identifies intellectual and moral reasoning applicable at different ages, and how these may affect children's behaviour and the manner in which teachers should respond to it. (We only refer to the first two levels of Kohlberg's model which incorporate four stages, as these are the stages relevant to school-aged children.)

Young children (5-6 year olds) are less able to understand the needs, and the points of view, of others. They are essentially egocentric and behave with little or no awareness of the impact of their behaviour on those around them. You need to be *quite direct and explicit* in your directions and instruction because children at these young ages do not have the level of cognitive development required to be persuaded by logical argument. Being at Stage One of moral reasoning, they tend to do things mainly to avoid punishment, rather than to preserve the rights of others. You need, therefore, to be quite direct. The very young child just needs to be told: "Sit down Andrew - stay in your seat while the TV is on."

As children move into middle childhood (ages 9-11) they become much more aware of rules and of socially appropriate behaviour. They need careful explanations in order to build up knowledge of what constitutes correct behaviour. Because they are becoming aware of the impact of their behaviour on others, and are also starting to be conscious of peer approval, they can often be managed by appealing to their need to be grown up, responsible and behave in order to please the peer group; for example, "Andrew, if you keep standing up, the other children can't see and that makes it hard for them to concentrate." That comment would be inappropriate for a 5-6 year old.

As adolescence emerges, communication skills involving problem solving, negotiation and recognition of maturity and responsibility should dominate. Adolescents need to be given explanations regarding the impact of their behaviour on others and those explanations need to be linked to an emotional level of experience. This is known as inductive reasoning. At this age, reprimands in front of peers are intensely embarrassing. The adolescent is far more likely to challenge you in order to be seen by the peer group as having some opinion; for example, "It wasn't just me who was talking ... there were others as well".

Table 1.1 Stages of Moral and Cognitive Development

Age	Stage of Cognitive Development (Piaget)	Stage of Moral Development (Kohlberg)	Issues in Classroom Management
2-6	**Preoperational Stage** Children are very egocentric; have difficulty distinguishing their point of view from that of others; are easily misled by surface appearances; are often confused about causal relationships	**Preconventional Level Stages 1 & 2** Children are obedient to authority in order to avoid punishment. Emphasis is on receiving rewards and avoiding punishments.	Children do what they want to with little awareness of the needs of others. Teachers need to be relatively direct.
6-12	**Concrete Operational Stage** Children are more capable of mental operations; can mentally separate, order and transform objects; still have considerable difficulty with abstract ideas and logical systematic thinking. Actions are still regarded as concrete.	**Conventional Level Stage 3** At 7-9 years, Stage 2 moral thinking slowly gives way to Stage 3; emphasis is on social acceptance; pleasing others and winning their praise and approval is more important than a specific reward; they are rapidly becoming more aware of peer influence.	Students of this age still need rules but are aware of looking foolish. Teachers can use group awareness to help manage the difficult child.
12-18	**Formal Operations Stage** Students can think systematically about problems and relationships. The ability to think in abstract terms develops.	**Conventional Level Stage 3 & 4** Most adolescents are still in Stage 3 where it is important to please significant others (usually peers). Later they will obey rules set by society and by individuals in power.	Students in Stage 3 are far less persuaded by power and position. They need to hear clear explanations and inductive logic. They are very sensitive to being reprimanded in front of peers...it is more effective to do it privately.

Note: Each of the stages outlined above must be considered approximate. Some children at 6-7 years are still in the preoperational stage, while another child at 5-6 years may have moved into the concrete operational stage. The same is also true for the other stages of cognitive and moral development.

When working with students throughout each of these stages, you should still maintain your role as limit setter, but the emphasis changes in each of the different stages. You need to continue to monitor each student's behaviour and apply gentle but firm correction of maladaptive behaviour.

Gender Differences

Gender differences are minimal in the infancy period but by 4-6 years of age, boys become less manageable and more active (Freiberg, 1992). At all ages past toddlerhood, research shows that boys are more likely to have problems at school and in adjustment (Baumrind, 1986). Boys have far more conduct problems, learning problems and attention problems (Carlson, Tamm & Gaub, 1997; Grainger, 1997). The socialisation practices used in rearing boys may be one of the most significant factors that create these differences.

Rate of maturation may be another important factor that creates a difference between the sexes. Boys are somewhat slower to develop than girls and there is the possibility that a percentage of boys are just not "ready" for school at five years of age (Carey & MacDevitt, 1978). Delayed entry may be advisable for some boys who are young entering school. It is preferable to hold a child back for a year than to let him enter school when not ready and experience some degree of failure. Because of this developmental difference, girls are often more able to benefit from exposure to a learning environment.

Physical and Sensory Abilities

Students have widely varying levels of physical co-ordination and abilities. Some students arrive at school unable to do up shoelaces or buttons. They may not have the dexterity to unwrap sandwiches carefully wrapped in plastic wrap by their mother (or father!), open their drink bottle or even open a lunchbox.

Differences in physical abilities and co-ordination continue until students leave school. Some have well-developed hand-eye co-ordination, have natural athletic abilities or physically mature earlier than their peers and star from an early age in games and sporting teams. Students who excel in games and sports are usually respected and liked by their peers and have an early advantage in finding their "place" at school. These children are unlikely to find less socially acceptable ways to find their place in the group.

Other students cannot walk past a desk without accidentally knocking something off, can't kick or throw a ball well, and have extremely untidy handwriting as a result of limited fine motor co-ordination. Poorly developed physical skills may be indicative of further developmental problems. These students begin with a disadvantage that may follow them throughout their school lives and require additional assistance or training from teachers to develop their physical abilities to an appropriate level.

In addition to differences in abilities that occur within "average" children, some students in regular schools now have significant disabilities. With the implementation of policies of integration and inclusion, all teachers can now expect to have students with a wide range of abilities and needs in their classrooms. The special schools which once catered for students with physical or sensory disabilities, now cater only for students with multiple and severe disabilities. It is an increasing trend for students with quite severe physical disabilities to be placed in the normalised environment of a regular school.

Students with significant hearing and vision impairments are also most often placed in regular classes. Although these students usually have the support of a specialist visiting teacher, they remain the ultimate responsibility of the class teacher, who must program, teach and evaluate the progress of these students just as she does for every other student. Students with physical and sensory impairments can certainly have an impact on how the classroom is physically arranged so all students have access to resources. Some of these students make quite extensive demands on teachers as additional services may need to be co-ordinated into the school day.

Cultural Background

Students may differ in their cultural background. In our multicultural society, some schools have students from many different nationalities. Formal education is valued in some cultures more than others; teachers and the authority invested in that role are accepted more widely in some cultures than others; asserting individual rights is more common practice in some cultures; and sharing materials and ideas is the way all issues and problems are solved in some societies, a practice that may clash with the individual effort required in external examinations.

These factors add to the complexity of the individual mix that comprises most classrooms. If they are not considered when planning teaching and classroom management strategies, it should not be surprising that problems occur.

Social Background

Some families will have the latest in information access via sophisticated technology. Some students will come from homes where reference books and literature from a wide range of sources are available and well used. Some students will have travelled widely, been on regular family holidays, and will have close relationships with immediate and extended family members. Some will have parents whose own school experiences were positive and so are cooperative and supportive of the school ethos.

Other students may come from families who have not had positive educational experiences. These families may have difficulty supporting the attitudes and habits you may be trying to develop in them. Some students may be required to organise younger siblings before school, prepare meals after school, care for a sick or disabled parent, work in a family business after school, or care for younger siblings because parents need to work and can't afford childcare. Some children may not have regular meals, may not have safe and secure home environments, and may even live with physical violence. These situations are not uncommon, and not unexpectedly, can have a great impact on class performance and behaviour. It is unfair and unrealistic to expect children with these background experiences to be as enthusiastic about learning and as willing to conform as some other students.

Temperament and Personality

We all know students who are engaging, cooperative and polite. These students have secure and stable pictures of themselves, and are able to interact confidently and appropriately with adults and children. They commonly attract the comment "a pleasure to teach" on their reports and are generally liked by teachers and peers.

Others students may be moody, irritable, and generally disliked. They may lack confidence, or appear shy and insecure. Some students are forever acting as the "class clown". Others may behave in an aggressive and intimidating manner.

What we know about each child's unique genetic inheritance suggests that there are temperament differences among children very early in life - in the first few weeks or even the first few days. Some babies are placid, others are excitable; some are introverted; others are extroverted. The work of Chess & Thomas (1996) and Sanson et al (1996) has clearly demonstrated that there are differences in the temperament of children even at these very early stages when environmental forces can hardly be said to have had any influence. The researchers were able to place newborn children into temperament categories on the basis of a range of characteristics such as activity levels, distractibility, quality of mood, adaptability and threshold of responsiveness. Around 12% of babies are described as having difficult temperaments and these patterns of behaviour tend to be quite consistent as the child grows up (Fergusson & Horwood, 1998).

Some babies are more placid, responsive and happy...

...than others!

A child with a difficult temperament may have a considerable impact on a teacher's sense of adequacy or self-efficacy. The difficult child will not respond as readily as other children do. He will be more unsettled and less inclined to follow rules. If you have one or more difficult children in your classroom, you will have significant problems managing the class due to differences in temperament and socialisation experiences. These factors can have a significant impact on the important process of developing positive relationships with some children. Strategies to overcome these are discussed in later chapters.

Cognitive Styles and Abilities

Even in streamed classes, there will be students with a range of cognitive abilities and potential. Some students will have better memories than others, and be able to process information more quickly and more effectively. Some will have a greater ability to manage the abstract notions that higher learning demands. Individual students may struggle in one area and have extraordinary talents in another.

Reports of the percentage of students who experience some degree of learning difficulties vary widely, depending on the definitions used and the specific area of difficulty. Estimates range from 5-20% (Andrews, Elkins, Berry & Burge, 1979), which means that most classes will have students who need some additional consideration. These difficulties are most often in the areas of reading, spelling and writing, all of which may be the result of underlying language-processing problems. Such fundamental problems often result in difficulties being experienced in other areas as most subjects, even mathematics, rely heavily on an understanding of the written word.

There is a clear link between learning difficulties and behaviour problems (Carroll, 1993; Edwards & Barkley, 1997; Hubbard & Newcomb, 1991; Landau & Milich, 1991; Shaywitz, Fletcher & Shaywitz, 1991, Trautman, Giddan & Jurs, 1990), as struggling in class can lead to feelings of low self-esteem. Students, it appears, would rather be seen to be "bad" than "stupid" and so learning problems are often masked behind an apparent lack of co-operation, an attitude of negativity or "couldn't care less".

The student with high levels of ability may prove equally as challenging as the student who struggles. Gifted students may be hypersensitive to criticism, intolerant of people who don't grasp concepts as easily as they do, argumentative and non-compliant (Silverman, 1994; Parker & Adkins, 1995). They are often easily bored by regular classroom activity (Landrum & Landrum, 1995). They require a creative and insightful teacher to ensure that the curriculum is meeting their needs. Gifted students may feel greatly "out of step" with their peers, which can lead to difficulties with social relationships and even classroom confrontations.

As well as differences in learning potential that will exist in most classrooms, students may differ in what is referred to as *cognitive style* (Wallace & McLoughlin, 1988). Some students may be highly impulsive, want to answer every question, be first in line, and so on. Some students may be more reflective, considering more alternatives before answering. Each of these differences has the potential to cause difficulties for a teacher who is not prepared for the diversity of abilities in today's classrooms.

Some Particular Conditions

In recent times, the occurrence of particular conditions associated with behaviour and management difficulties in school-aged children has received considerable attention. The diagnosis of such conditions as Asperger's Syndrome, Attention Deficit Hyperactivity Disorder (ADHD), Oppositional Defiant Disorder (ODD) and Conduct Disorder (CD) has increased. Each of these conditions increases a student's predisposition to behavioural problems, and teachers need to be familiar with their key characteristics, and the sorts of management approaches which have been successful in managing them. For this reason, we will spend a little time discussing these diagnoses now, with particular reference to how these conditions may affect classroom behaviour.

We will not be discussing detailed management strategies in this chapter, but will refer in forthcoming chapters to strategies or adaptations to strategies that are particularly appropriate for students with the following diagnoses.

Asperger's Syndrome

A term that is appearing more and more on student record files is Asperger's Syndrome (or Asperger's Disorder). It is sometimes referred to as "high functioning autism". Both autism and Asperger's Syndrome share the core features of impaired social interaction; repetitive, stereotypical patterns of behaviour and activities; inflexible thinking; and lack of imaginative play (Wing & Gould, 1979). Although regarded as being part of the Autistic Spectrum Disorders, Asperger's Syndrome does not include the same language and communication difficulties that help define autism (Frith, 1991).

Characteristics of Asperger's Syndrome

Normal to above IQ and communication

Unlike most students with conventional autism (Kanner's Syndrome) who have some intellectual disability, most students with Asperger's Syndrome have normal to above average IQ (Cumine, Leach & Stevenson, 1998; Frith, 1991).

Lack of social-interaction skills

Although children with Asperger's Syndrome may relate quite normally to family members, they have difficulty with social cues and a poor understanding of non-verbal communication skills such as facial expressions, gestures and body language. They tend to engage in repetitive patterns of behaviour which people often find disturbing, hence social interactions are affected. Their often pedantic, robotic, formal sounding language adds to their social interaction difficulties (Jordan & Powell, 1995; Wing, 1996).

Egocentricity; lack of empathy

Students with Asperger's find it difficult to understand the emotions and reactions of other people. While wanting to engage in social interactions, their lack of social skills and inability to empathise makes this very difficult. They tend to interact to meet their own needs, but find the social demands of others hard to meet (Frith, 1991; Wing, 1996).

Superficial language comprehension

Initially communication skills appear to develop normally, but it becomes apparent that language comprehension is very superficial and operates at only the concrete level (Attwood, 1998; Frith, 1991).

Extreme interests and routines

The obsessive interests and ritualistic behaviour of students with Asperger's Syndrome appear to be attempts to make sense of the world. Gaining a great deal of information and talking about a particular topic allows them to impose order on the world. They are resistant to change as change brings with it confusion and disorder. Comfort and safety exist in familiar routines (Attwood, 1998; Frith, 1991).

Motor co-ordination problems

Students with Asperger's often have both gross and fine motor co-ordination problems. An odd gait and awkward posture are commonly noted. They find handwriting difficult so written tasks are often left unfinished. They have organisational problems, finding it difficult to find materials or be in the right place at the right time (Richard,1997).

Incidence

A prevalence rate of 36 per 10,000 has been quoted by Ehlers and Gillberg (1993) with the probable ratio of boys to girls being 10 -15:1.

Assessment

Like ADHD, there is no convenient blood test, brain scan or even a single behaviour that will conclusively identify Asperger's Syndrome. The diagnosis is established by observation of a pattern of behaviours by an experienced clinician using interviews and rating scales. Individual behaviours can vary enormously, but they all seem to fall within the categories of behaviour described previously: difficulties with social interaction; poor social communication and social imagination; inflexible thinking; and lack of creative play. Assessment information needs to be gathered sensitively and needs to occur across contexts (Cumine, Leach & Stevenson, 1998).

Causes

Asperger's Syndrome is thought to have some genetic basis, with members of the same family often being seen as eccentric or "odd". Asperger's is probably the result of several "triggers", rather than a single cause. Sometimes birth complications, viral infections or other causes of brain trauma have been evident in individuals with Asperger's Syndrome. It is described as a brain dysfunction, but the precise areas of the brain involved are not known (Gillberg & Coleman, 1992; Trevarthen, Aitken, Papoudi & Robarts, 1996).

Related Problems

ADHD is often diagnosed with Asperger's, with the ADHD diagnosis usually being made first. Attention problems and hyperactivity are the most obvious shared characteristics and these can lead to further learning difficulties. The mental rigidity of students with Asperger's means that they have difficulty with such things as metaphors and humour, and have trouble transferring and generalising information. They will misinterpret abstract or figurative information (Frith, 1991).

At adolescence, these students become aware of the fact that their peers have friendships but they are unable to establish and maintain friendships successfully themselves. Emotional problems, particularly anxiety attacks and depression often arise as a result.

In future chapters, we will be discussing teaching and management strategies that you can use to help students with Asperger's Syndrome. Many of the effective teaching strategies are useful for these students, although they will need additional considerations in some areas (Attwood, 1998; Frith, 1991; Gilbert, 1996).

Attention Deficit Hyperactivity Disorder (ADHD)

Behaviours similar to those associated with Attention Deficit Hyperactivity Disorder have been noted for over a hundred years (Still, 1902). Terms such as *brain damage* (Werner and Strauss, 1941); *minimal brain damage* (Laufer & Denhoff, 1957); *minimal brain dysfunction (MBD)* (Clements & Peters, 1962) and *hyperkinetic reaction of childhood* (American Psychiatric Association, 1968) have been used to describe conditions characterised by hyperactivity, restlessness, distractibility and attention problems.

Characteristics of ADHD

Attention Problems

Students with ADHD have difficulty screening out irrelevant information. They find listening and following instructions difficult, especially if there is a great deal of other activity going on in the classroom simultaneously. They can, however, pay attention more easily to new, colourful or moving stimuli. This is why such students enjoy, and can pay attention to, computer games such as Nintendo. It is also why their attention is so easily distracted by moving objects such as items hanging down from the ceiling in classrooms.

Students with ADHD have attention difficulties

Increased Motor Activity or Hyperactivity

Students with this component seem unable to keep still. They wriggle, move out of their seats, talk excessively (and usually loudly) and fidget with anything available. They either take the "scenic route" when moving about the classroom, talking to other students, touching things, flicking rulers off desks, etc on the way, or take the shortest possible route, running, jumping over chairs and so on. They rarely complete set tasks, but rather switch rapidly from one task to another. These behaviours are some of the most frustrating for teachers because they usually distract the whole class.

Impulsivity

Students with this characteristic often interrupt, call out answers and have great difficulty waiting for teacher attention or for their turn in a game. They rarely read instructions before commencing a task. Because they don't develop planning skills or establish routines, equipment, books and homework are often lost or poorly organised. Impulsivity often results in students doing physically dangerous things, because they do not stop to consider the consequences of their actions (Zentall, 1993).

ADHD as an umbrella term

Attention Deficit Hyperactivity Disorder (ADHD) is now the umbrella term for a number of different conditions. Diagnostic criteria are found in Box 1.1. The latest edition of the Diagnostic and Statistical Manual of Mental Disorders (DSM-IV, 1994) identifies three subtypes within ADHD:

> Type 1 ADHD-IA The main feature of Type 1 is inattention. Students with this are often referred to as "dreamy" and do not demonstrate the hyperactivity and impulsivity usually associated with ADHD.
> Type 2 ADHD-HI Individuals with this type are both hyperactive and impulsive but do not experience attention problems.
> Type 3 ADHD Combined subtype. This diagnosis includes children who are inattentive, hyperactive and impulsive.

These subtypes, however, are usually not made clear in reports and the broad label ADHD is used to cover all subtypes. In order for this diagnosis to be made, the symptoms need to be present across contexts and have been evident from a young age (usually first noted between the ages of two and four years). It is also a requirement of a diagnosis of ADHD that the symptoms cannot be explained by other factors such as major environmental problems or emotional disturbance and that they should be serious enough to cause difficulties in the child's and family's (and eventually the teacher's!) life (American Psychiatric Association, 1994).

Incidence

Most recent and reliable research reports an incidence of 3-4% of the school-age population (Carmichael et al, 1997). There is a higher incidence in males than females, ranging from 3:1 to 9:1.

Assessment

Unfortunately there is no simple and foolproof way of diagnosing this condition. Many professionals believe that ADHD is over-diagnosed. Diagnosis should only occur after information has been gathered from various sources, mostly using behavioural checklists similar to that seen in

Box 1.1. Teachers are often called upon to complete such a checklist. The severity of the behaviours and any co-existing problems should be noted.

Box 1.1 Diagnostic Criteria for Attention Deficit Hyperactivity Disorder

Six or more of the following symptoms of inattention have persisted for at least 6 months to a degree which is maladaptive and inconsistent with developmental level.

Inattention
- a) Often fails to give close attention to details or makes careless mistakes in schoolwork, work or other activities.
- b) Often has difficulty sustaining attention in tasks or play activities.
- c) Often does not seem to pay attention when spoken to directly.
- d) Often does not follow through on instructions and fails to finish schoolwork, chores, or duties in the workplace.
- e) Often has difficulty organising tasks and activities.
- f) Often avoids, dislikes or is reluctant to engage in tasks that require sustained mental effort.
- g) Often loses things necessary for tasks or activities.
- h) Is often easily distracted by extraneous stimuli.
- i) Is often forgetful in daily activities.

Six or more of the following symptoms of hyperactivity-impulsivity have persisted for at least 6 months to a degree which is maladaptive and inconsistent with developmental level

Hyperactivity
- a) Often fidgets with hands or feet or squirms in seat.
- b) Often leaves seat in classroom or in other situations in which remaining in seat is expected.
- c) Often runs about or climbs excessively in situations in which it is inappropriate.
- d) Often has difficulty playing or engaging in leisure activities quietly.
- e) Is often "on the go" or often acts as if "driven by a motor".
- f) Often talks excessively.

Impulsivity
- g) Often blurts out answers before questions have been completed.
- h) Often has difficulty awaiting turn.
- i) Often interrupts or intrudes on others.

(American Psychiatric Association, 1994)

Proposed Causes

It is now generally believed that ADHD is caused by a variation or a malfunction of the neurobiological system (Barkley, 1990; Carroll, 1993; Ellard, 1993; Goldstein, 1995; Hynd, Hern, Voeller, & Marshall, 1991; Pelligrini & Horvat, 1995), although there are a number of different explanations of the precise way in which this occurs.

The neuro-chemical explanation of ADHD proposes that the behaviours associated with ADHD occur because the central nervous system – the brain – cannot produce enough of the family of chemical neurotransmitters called the catecholamines (Zametkin & Rapoport, 1987). Within this group of neurotransmitters the most important for the regulation of attention, impulsivity and motor responses are norepinephrine and dopamine. A deficiency in the production of these two neurotransmitters occurs within the brain stem causing decreased stimulation of the cells and thus a dysfunction of the neural pathways (Goldstein, 1995; Hynd et al, 1991). It is the dysfunction of the neural pathways that causes the impulsivity, restlessness and inattentiveness which characterise Attention Deficit Hyperactivity Disorder.

Other proposed causes include differences in brain structure identified by newly developed technology, such as magnetic resonance imaging (MRI) (Hynd et al, 1991) and positron emission tomography (PET) (Zametkin & Rapoport, 1987).

There is strong research evidence from family history and twin studies that there is a genetic factor in ADHD (Barkley, 1990; Faraone et al, 1993; Friedman & Doyal, 1992; Levy, Hay & McLaughlin, 1996; Levy, Hay & McStephen, 1997; Parker, 1992). Many parents of children diagnosed with ADHD recognise behaviours of their own, or of family members. It is not unusual for parents to be diagnosed and even to begin taking medication after their children have been diagnosed.

There is no clinical evidence that special diets help most students diagnosed with ADHD, although a very small percentage (less than 5%) of children diagnosed with ADHD may be affected by artificial dietary additives and so benefit from restricted diets (Carmichael et al, 1997; Carroll, 1993; Forness, Kavale, Blum, & Lloyd, 1997). Diets which rely on megadoses of vitamins have not been found to be widely effective and also carry the risk of toxicity.

Barkley (1990) claims that ADHD can also be related to pregnancy or birth complications, or can develop from disease or trauma to the central nervous system. External environmental factors may also be of significance. Certain contexts appear to be more problematic for these children than others. Classrooms which lack stimulation, chaotic or disorganised home environments, child abuse and neglect can exacerbate the difficulties these children face (Carroll, 1993), but there is no convincing evidence that the external environment itself is a causal factor (Barkley, 1990).

Related Problems

Learning difficulties, including reading disabilities (up to 30%) and spelling and mathematics problems (10-15%) are often associated with this diagnosis (August & Garfinkel, 1990; Fergusson & Horwood, 1992; Lerner et al, 1995; Scruggs & Mastropieri, 1992; Shaywitz et al, 1992; Zentall, 1993) .

Behavioural problems have also been widely associated with ADHD (Bailey & Rice, 1997; Carmichael et al, 1997; Carroll, 1993; Cooper & Ideus, 1995; Hinshaw, 1992; Reid et al, 1993; Young-Loveridge, 1997). These learning and behavioural difficulties can lead to a range of other problems for diagnosed students. Poor motivation, low self-esteem and social rejection are widely reported. Antisocial, oppositional, aggressive and even violent behaviours occur in 40-60% of students diagnosed with ADHD (Anastopoulos & Barkley, 1992).

Stimulant medication

Many students with a diagnosis of ADHD benefit from prescribed medication. Stimulant medication, such as Ritalin (methylphenidate) and Dexedrine (dextro amphetamine), is the most widely used of all treatments. Psychostimulant medication increases the production of norepinephrine, which normalises the levels of neurotransmitters and allows them to perform their function of moderating impulses and monitoring attention (Hynd et al, 1991; Pelham et al, 1990). Medication of this nature results in temporary increases in attention, social adjustment and a temporary decrease in impulsivity, but doesn't contribute to teaching or teach pro-social behaviour. Possible side effects include depression, growth retardation, sleep disturbances, insomnia, weight loss, irritability, increased heart rate, and development of Tourette's Syndrome (tics).

The strategies we discuss Chapters Five and Six are useful for students with ADHD. We have also included in those chapters specific strategies which research has been found to be particularly useful for students with ADHD.

Oppositional Defiant Disorder (ODD)

Some students differ in their tolerance of frustration and willingness to persevere when they do not get their own way or when understanding does not come quickly or easily. Some students appear to have a "short fuse", move off task quickly and behave in an aggressive and hostile manner.

When a child's behaviour becomes extremely difficult both at school and at home he may be identified as having Oppositional Defiant Disorder (ODD). Oppositional Disorder is not a defined medical condition. It is usually characterised by several behaviours that cluster together rather than just one very intense behaviour.

Characteristics almost universally accepted with ODD include defiance, tantrums, non-compliance, aggression and some degree of destructiveness. The behaviours that make up Oppositional Defiant Disorder are listed below.

Box 1.2 Diagnostic Criteria for Oppositional Defiant Disorder

a) Often loses temper.
b) Often argues with adults.
c) Often actively defies or refuses adult requests or rules.
d) Often deliberately annoys other people.
e) Often blames others for his or her own mistakes.
f) Is often touchy or easily annoyed by others.
g) Is often angry and resentful.
h) Is often spiteful or vindictive.
(American Psychiatric Association, 1994)

Some students actively defy adult requests

In order to distinguish these behaviours from normal displays of temper, aggression, and so on, three criteria need to be considered.

> - **Problem Frequency** This refers to the number of times the student repeats a particular undesirable behaviour. Sometimes a particular behaviour is considered to be trivial, but if it occurs repeatedly it can be considered a problem. Frequency needs to be judged in relation to an average child in the grade – the behaviour needs to be occurring much more often than normal.
> - **Problem Duration** If a problem behaviour has existed for an extended time the criterion of duration is met. If a behaviour occurs following some stressful situation and lasts only a few days or a few weeks, it would not meet the criteria for duration. Once an unwarranted behaviour has been established for at least a month the criteria of duration has been met.
> - **Problem Intensity** The child that calls out can be a problem but the child who screams loudly and is excessively demanding would meet the condition of intensity. Once again, the comparison group is normal peers and the concept of intensity is related to the high level of demanding or negative behaviour. Sometimes behaviours do not meet the criteria for frequency or duration, but meet the criteria of intensity. Examples of such behaviours might be throwing rocks at other children, using a large stick as a weapon, or inappropriate touching of other children. Such behaviours are deemed so inappropriate and outside the range of normal behaviour that the criterion of intensity is satisfied.

Causes

It is thought that ODD arises as a combination of a genetic predisposition, such as a low frustration tolerance or poor anger management, which is then triggered by environmental factors such as an influential peer group or a particularly frustrating environment. Parental alcoholism, restrictive parenting, substance abuse and mood disorders have all been associated with ODD, although not exclusively. While ODD can be present in any ethnic and social background, it is more prevalent among children from lower socio-economic households (Simonoff, Pickles, Meyer, Silberg & Maes, 1998).

Medication is used if ODD co-occurs with conditions like depression, tics or seizure disorders. It is also used if symptoms are very severe, although gaining the co-operation of the student concerned is often difficult, as non co-operation is part of the problem (Steiner et al, 1997).

Related Problems

There is a significant overlap of oppositional disorders and other problems. ADHD and depression/anxiety disorders occur in significant numbers. Learning problems also occur in large numbers (Bernstein, 1996; Kuhne, Schachar & Tannock, 1997; Steiner et al, 1997).

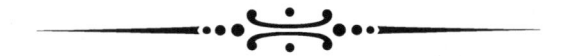

Conduct Disorder (CD)

The term Conduct Disorder usually applies to older children who have progressed from early ODD. As they have grown older they have become more difficult to manage and increasingly anti-social. Unfortunately, unless treated, over 50% of 6-7 year olds (Batton & Russell, 1995; Barkley, 1987; Jessor & Jessor, 1977) who display oppositional behaviour fail to grow out of it in adolescence and move on to more serious behaviours. A student may be identified as Conduct Disordered if three or more of the following criteria exist:

Box 1.3 Diagnostic Criteria for Conduct Disorder

Aggression to people and animals
- a) Often bullies, threatens or intimidates others.
- b) Often initiates physical fights.
- c) Has used a weapon that can cause serious physical harm to others (for example, a bat, brick, broken bottle, knife, gun).
- d) Has been physically cruel to people.
- e) Has been physically cruel to animals.
- f) Has stolen while confronting a victim (for example, mugging, purse snatching, extortion, armed robbery).
- g) Has forced someone into sexual activity.

Destruction of property
- h) Has deliberately engaged in fire setting with the intent of causing serious damage.
- i) Has deliberately destroyed others' property (other than by fire setting).

Deceitfulness or theft
- j) Has broken into someone else's house, building or car.
- k) Often lies to obtain goods or favours or to avoid obligation (i.e., "cons" others).
- l) Has stolen items of non-trivial value without confronting a victim (e.g., shoplifting, but without breaking and entering; forgery).

Serious violation of rules
- m) Often stays out at night despite parental prohibitions.
- n) has run away from home overnight at least twice while living in parental or parental surrogate home (or once without returning for a lengthy period).
- o) Often truants from school.

(American Psychiatric Association, 1994)

Incidence

Studies that estimate the number of children with conduct disorders in the general population are quite consistent, ranging from 5.5% – 7% (Connell, Irvine & Rodney, 1982; Offord, Boyle & Racene, 1989; Satterfield, Hoppe & Schell, 1982).

Related problems

Conduct disorder can occur with 20-40% of students with ADHD (Szatmari, Offord & Boyle, 1989). It is clear from these characteristics that conduct disordered children and adolescents place themselves at risk for a range of educational, legal and psychological problems and they will need extra help to learn the pro-social skills that most children possess (Kuhne, Schachar & Tannock, 1997).

Students with oppositional and conduct disorders are very difficult to manage in the classroom. Indeed, many of them do not remain in the regular classroom, but require individualised programs in more specialised settings. If they are to remain in regular classes, meeting their needs requires careful planning, and the use of incentive schemes and individual behaviour programs. We describe these in Chapters Six and Seven.

Conclusion

The ways in which students may differ is almost inexhaustible. You cannot expect the same attitudes from all students towards learning and all it entails: application to class tasks, acceptance of teacher directions, homework, study, and so on. In general, teachers who understand and allow for these individual differences in their preparation, their management and their responses to individual behaviour are most likely to have cooperative classes with few management difficulties.

Chapter Two

CREATING A POSITIVE LEARNING ENVIRONMENT

Introduction

There is no doubt that when you walk into a classroom, you are aware of the "tone", or feeling that is present. This usually, but not always, has something to do with the physical arrangement of the classroom, classroom decoration and so on. It always has something to do with how engaged the students are in what they are doing and in their general demeanour.

This chapter will explore different aspects of a positive learning environment. We will look at:

> ➢ **The Physical Setting of the Classroom**
> ➢ **The Emotional Climate of the Classroom**

The Physical Setting

The physical environment you establish for your students communicates a great deal about your expectations. There will be elements of your immediate teaching environment that you will not be able to control. If you are a new arrival at the school, you (unfortunately) may well be allocated the worst or the most isolated room. Primary teachers have an overwhelming advantage in that they usually have their "own" room. Most secondary teachers will not have their own teaching space, but there are still strategies you can use to create an environment that encourages co-operation and reduces conflict. Even if you are sharing teaching space, most teachers will not object to an improvement in their teaching environment. There is also much less likelihood of vandalism or accidental damage by the students if the classroom decoration has been initiated by, and in part belongs to, the students themselves.

Desk Arrangements

Think carefully about where and how students will be seated. Seating arrangements which allow the teacher to see the faces of all students at all times have been associated with increased academic engaged time (Askew, 1993; Bender & Mathes, 1995; Christenson et al, 1987; Hudson, 1997; Mathes & Fuchs, 1994). It is easier to attract and maintain the students' attention in these positions. Proximity control (moving close to students who are off task) is one of the most low-key and effective behaviour management strategies. This means that you must be able to move freely around the classroom, so that you can reach all students easily, especially those who will require your attention regularly.

Tables in rows, small clusters, larger blocks, U-shapes or work stations all have advantages and disadvantages. Each style of desk arrangement will encourage certain behaviours and discourage others.

If you have tables in groups, with students facing each other, you are more likely to have student interaction and talk. This is exactly what you want in some lessons, but perhaps not in others. Off-task student interaction is far more likely to occur with desks in groups; it is harder to gain eye contact; and noise levels will almost definitely be higher. If groups of tables are used, it is important that the students are still able to see you without physically turning for those occasions when you need to speak to the whole class.

Desks placed in single or double rows are useful for teacher demonstrations and independent seatwork. Desks placed in this more formal manner suggest order and task focus. It is easier for the teacher to gain eye contact with all students and to monitor student activity. This arrangement is less likely to encourage student-to-student interaction. If you are having trouble settling the class down, this arrangement is recommended until the students learn greater self-management skills.

U-shaped arrangements are often a good compromise. Students can have eye contact with all other students for class discussions, but the eye contact is at a greater distance and therefore less likely to encourage private discussions. Tables can be moved easily for group work when necessary. Unfortunately, many classrooms are not large enough for a single U-shape, and a double U-shape eliminates eye-contact between some students.

A workstation arrangement requires students to have well developed self-management skills. It is far harder for a teacher to gain eye-contact, and to monitor the activity of each student. Students do not have their own individual space with this arrangement, which is a problem for some. You still need to have some defined space for whole-class instruction. This arrangement, however, is very useful for students who can work co-operatively and who have a strong "group" feeling. It is not recommended if there are any very difficult students in the class, or if management problems are an issue. This arrangement often works well towards the end of a year, when a strong group feeling has developed, when the students can work independently and co-operatively, and when there are no serious management issues.

Re-establishing Control

Changing the seating is an excellent way to re-establish control if this is necessary. You may want to change seating arrangements when you start a new unit which requires different working patterns. When deciding on your desk configuration and room arrangement, you should carefully consider:

- where students will keep their personal belongings;
- where student notebooks, folders, etc will be kept;
- where class resources should be located, especially those that are likely to be accessed frequently, and those that have the potential to be highly distracting (like electric pencil sharpeners).

Student placement

Think about where easily distracted students should be placed. Classroom-based research suggests such students should be seated away from doorways and windows and away from each other, but relatively close to you. They should not be seated near high-traffic areas such as student lockers or tubs, or resources that are accessed frequently.

Having a distractible or hyperactive student in the middle at the front of the room often occurs but this is not recommended. The movement and activity associated with such a student can be a major distraction to the rest of the class. On one side of the room, close to the front is a position that is generally recommended for students with attention problems. The student is then out of the direct line of vision of most students during whole-class instruction but this placement still allows easy access by the teacher.

Decoration

Students like to see their own high quality work displayed, even in secondary school. Younger students (and some older) like their own photographs incorporated in classroom displays, such as birthday charts, monitor charts, group identifiers, lifelines, etc. A class banner, perhaps with motto and photographs of class members, can be part of a positive and welcoming entrance to your classroom.

Secondary students may prefer environmental posters (rainforest scenes, landscapes, endangered species, dolphins, eagles, etc), or some of the many humorous (but still tasteful!) posters that are available now.

Class-made posters help students develop a sense of belonging to the classroom. Banners with inspirational quotes, and display boards on which students can attach jokes or cartoons (after some discreet vetting!) are also popular in secondary classrooms. Class-made murals or collages related to a unit of study are also an attractive part of many classrooms.

Plants can have a positive effect on the physical appearance of the least appealing room, and can be a useful aid in developing responsibility in those who care for them.

Animals

Fish, birds, tadpoles, mice and a number of other species can add novelty and colour (and often noise, odour and other less wanted additions!) but they do come with a great responsibility for their care. These are very popular in junior classrooms and can help develop responsibility, but should not be in any classroom where they are likely to be hurt or neglected.

Music

Music can be a great addition to a classroom. A "personal choice" piece can be a reward for individuals or groups at certain times of the day, or music can be played as background to seatwork. This is a great opportunity to broaden the musical experiences of your students (and often yourself when it comes to student choice, especially in secondary classrooms!)

The Emotional Climate

Most educators acknowledge that the emotional tone of the classroom is very important in promoting learning (Glasser, 1993; Goldstein, 1995; Jones, 1987a, 1987b; Rogers, 1995; Ruddell, 1995).

Box 2.1 Teachers are Important

> I cannot think of any successful person who, when giving biographical information, has not credited a teacher's influence for contributing significantly to his or her accomplishments. What is singled out is not usually the knowledge that that teacher imparted, but rather the impact of his or her personality that permanently altered the student's outlook... What makes the difference is that as a result of their relationship the student's view of himself is permanently altered. (Basch, 1989, p.773-4)

The emotional bond that you develop with your students can contribute greatly to their learning, and to their development as individuals. You have the power to make a year greatly enjoyable, or quite miserable for each student in your class. Those of you who are parents of school-aged children, think about how anxiously you wait to hear which teacher your child has for the year. Although teachers' salaries and status may have declined in recent years, you are nevertheless very powerful figures when one considers the significance you have in so many children's lives.

We believe that the emotional bond that can exist between student and teacher has particular significance for students with management and behavioural problems. We discussed in Chapter One the characteristics of students with ADHD. Professor Russell Barkley (2001) has spoken of these students as having a motivation deficit. They have enormous problems dealing with any sense of the future: they are "here and now" students. Homework, future assignments, etc are not within their scope of thinking. In order for these students to maintain attention, to work consistently on assignments, and to undergo the boredom associated with practice of repetitive tasks, they need an additional motivator. In many cases, this motivator can be the relationship they have with their teacher. It is far easier to pay attention to someone we really like, or admire, or love. We want their approval. We listen to what they say. We do what they want us to do. There is less effort involved than in doing these things for someone we find boring or irritating. The bond you share with your students can act as a great motivator, encouraging the student to pay attention, even if only to win your approval.

For students with conditions like Asperger's, who may be socially isolated from peers, a bond with the teacher can encourage, inspire, and otherwise greatly assist. Such students are quite vulnerable to depression, and the relationship aspect of the classroom may be an important aspect of enabling these students to persevere.

Oppositional and conduct-disordered students also need a great advocate in the classroom. These students cause a great deal of stress and disharmony, but need to know that you are "on their side". They will continue to test your management skills, but if they are convinced that you believe in them, and want them to achieve, you have a far greater chance of becoming that person who can really connect with them. This personal connection can be the factor that really turns that life around.

How can you develop a close bond with your students? You need to find ways to let each student know that he or she is respected and acknowledged as an individual. While being an individual becomes almost the "raison d'etre" (the reason for existence) of adolescents, it is also important for younger students. Even as adults, we appreciate it when we are acknowledged as an individual in some way. This is certainly part of what Glasser (1993) refers to when stating that we all have a need for freedom to be seen as an individual, rather than only as a member of a group.

Strategies for Creating a Positive Emotional Climate

Greet students personally

Greeting students personally each day is a good start. This means that you have to be in the room before school or the period starts – not always possible but a good aim. Saying the student's name, a nod in their direction, a reference to a new hair colour, joggers, (body piercing?), a query about the new baby at home, or about how their team went over the weekend are all signs that you are recognising each person as an individual and care enough to acknowledge that. When this becomes part of the routine, the students will recognise that this is not the time for a lengthy response.

Make frequent eye contact

Try to make eye contact with every student every day. This is difficult, especially for secondary teachers who may have over a hundred different students in classes in a single day. Nevertheless, eye contact increases the connection between people, and this is exactly what you are trying to do.

Negotiate rules and routines with students

We will be talking more specifically about how to develop rules and routines in Chapter Three, but an important aspect of them is that they be developed through negotiation with the students. Students must feel some sense of ownership if they are to "take them on board". This relates to Glasser's (1993) belief that we all have a need for power. You are making a powerful statement to students if you say that you trust their collective wisdom enough for them to take part in deciding how the classroom will operate.

Acknowledge positive behaviours

Teachers are usually quick to point out when students do the wrong thing. It is just as important (if not more so) to acknowledge when they are doing the right thing. This applies particularly to those occasions when you see students sharing belongings or equipment, looking after each other, inviting a new student to join an activity, apologising, resolving an argument or helping out in some way. Many opportunities to build a positive classroom climate are missed if acts such as these pass unacknowledged.

Use positive language

This means more than the usual "Catch them being good" tip. It takes a bit of practice, but most negative statements can be turned into positive ones. Consider the difference between the following responses:

> Student: Miss, can we have a game of *Buzz Off*?
> Response 1: No, because we haven't finished our maths yet.
>
> or
>
> Response 2: Yes, as soon as we have finished our maths.

"Yes, when..." promotes a much more positive tone than "no, because" or "not until". Try to answer as many questions as possible with "Yes, ..." even if it's nothing more than "Yes, at the end of the week when...".

Similar advice may be considered when attempting to direct students to stop doing things. "No running inside" is easily translated into "Walking inside...thanks". (We like Bill Rogers' (1990) use of "thanks" after requests rather than "please" because it assumes compliance). Often students are told what *not* to do, but this is rarely followed up by a positive direction as to what they *should* be doing.

Interact with students outside the classroom

This doesn't mean deliberately involving yourself in all their social activities (as if they'd let you!) but it does mean a smile as you pass in the corridor or at the local shopping centre.

This can also be one very useful positive outcome of playground duty (and the more positives we can find about this the better because it is one of the most unpopular aspects of teaching for most teachers). Playground duty gives you the opportunity to interact on a more informal level with the students, without the constraints and demands of a syllabus interfering. This is when you are more likely to find out what the students did at the weekend, whose family is expecting a new baby, who has just received their driving licence (it's good to be warned!) who the smokers are, what the favourite television show is, which is the current "cool" radio station, what kind of music they like and a myriad of other titbits of information that will help you understand where your students are "coming from".

Minimise embarrassment

There will be times when you need to point out to students that their behaviour is not acceptable, but it should always be done in a way that allows students to "save face". Reasonable requests are more likely to be met than demands. You can expect an apology, but you cannot demand one. It is extremely difficult to force someone, once past the age of about two, to do something she is determined not to do. (Have you ever tried to get a two and a half year old, who is determined not to, into the bath? The point is made!)

Use humour

Some teachers have the gift (and it is a gift) of being able to defuse the threatening situation, of getting the difficult student to do something no-one else can, through the use of humour. Not everyone can be as quick off the mark as we would like. But we can all practise taking (some) things less seriously and allowing humour to ease us through the day.

Use bibliotherapy

Bibliotherapy has been a useful strategy to improve behaviour in students from grades 3 to 12 (Bauer & Balius, 1995; Goldstein, 1995; McCarty & Chalmers, 1997; Pardeck & Markward, 1994). This strategy uses books at the appropriate reading and developmental levels which address an issue confronting a class. Such issues might include bullying, shyness, or problems getting along with others. The student(s) must be able to see similarities between themselves and the book character in order to identify with the character and relate to the situation described in the story. As the students become aware that the problem they are experiencing is the same as the book character, some level of insight occurs. They realise that the problems they are experiencing are not unique, need not remain static, and may be resolved. Alternative behaviours are explored and often adopted.

Bibliotherapy can enhance self-understanding, self esteem and greater acceptance of individual differences if used correctly. It requires the teacher to select books carefully and guide discussions during reading in order to help students identify with the characters, situations and resolutions in the book. Guidelines for using bibliotherapy are detailed in Sridhar & Vaughan (2000).

Use Class Meetings

Class meetings can be used in a variety of ways to add to the emotional climate of a classroom. Glasser (1969) has been advocating these for more than three decades, but they are a vastly under-utilised resource in most classrooms. If this is done on a regular basis, it creates a sense of belonging and promotes group feeling.

Class meetings are different from other sorts of class-based discussions. They are held in a circle. Even the very act of changing the seating arrangements in the room signifies the fact that a different form of communication is about to take place. There should be an agenda and a clear understanding of how individuals should participate.

Class meetings can be used to resolve an immediate social problem, to discuss some academic issue, or to provide a forum of discussion on any relevant issue that the students wish to raise. It may be a classroom issue or it may address an issue that takes place outside the classroom, such as bullying.

Box 2.2 Addressing Bullying through Class Meetings

One way of combating bullying behaviour is to have a class discussion about this topic. An important aspect of bullying is that it is usually a hidden or covert activity. This is part of the intimidation – it occurs when protection is not available for the victim. The simple act of talking about it – bringing the topic into the open – can be an important first step. It alerts everyone to its existence and increases the chance that the victim may have support when it occurs. It also alerts any bullies in the class that their behaviour has been noted and is being taken seriously.

Have a discussion about what bullying is. Important concepts include that:
- it is when a stronger, more powerful person hurts or frightens a weaker or smaller person;
- it is an inappropriate use of power;
- it is deliberate;
- it is repeated.

It is not
- just boys who bully;
- just teasing;
- weak to report bullies;
- something that will necessarily stop if you ignore it.

You could discuss bullying behaviours with your class. Include such things as embarrassing people and making people feel uncomfortable, breaking their things, making people feel inferior and spreading rumours as well as the more overt behaviours. The class could discuss reasons they think bullying occurs and how it could be combated.

Classroom Activities to Build Self Esteem and a Feeling of Belonging

For younger classes

Class Post box

For Grades 1- 4, a class post box can be very useful. Students can write to each other or to you. Try to write a short note to at least one student each week. Write a letter to a student who does not normally receive any letters. Once a week, open the box and deliver the mail. This gives you a chance to remind students that you have a greater chance of receiving mail if you write to other people.

Class Coat of Arms or Flag

Use a template of a traditional coat of arms, a shield or a flag, to describe qualities you want your class to reflect and mount it on the classroom door, facing outwards so visitors can see it.

Silhouettes

Working in pairs, students draw silhouettes of each other using sheets of butcher's paper and the light source coming from an overhead projector. Students then cover their individual silhouettes with images, words, etc that they believe help make them the person they are. These may be depictions of hobbies, words cut from magazines, and newspaper headlines that are of interest or concern to them.

Class Joke Book

Develop a class joke book that is added to on a regular basis. You will need to monitor the jokes that are entered to ensure that there are no racist or sexist jokes.

Barrel of Laughs

Place jokes written on slips of paper in a barrel shaped container. Draw one out and share it with the class as a transition activity or at the end of the day.

The One and Only...

Distribute index cards to students on which they write three sentences about themselves. The aim is to describe themselves but not make it too easy or too hard to guess who the description fits. Ask the students to include a unique feature, experience or talent – the things that make each of them unique. Cards are then collected, shuffled and handed out to the group. Students take it in turns to read out the card they received, and guess who it describes.

Unfinished business

Write a series of sentence beginnings on separate cards. Some suggested beginnings are:
- I wish I knew……..
- I am scared of……..
- If I were older, I would…….
- My favourite memory is……
- I like it when other people in the class…..

Distribute the cards in small groups and the students select one and complete the sentence. Allow the students to indicate if they would like the "unfinished business" to be shared with the class or not.

Making Teams

This activity points out that, although we are all unique in some ways, we also share many attributes. Draw up a chart of various "teams" that exist in the class. This activity can also be done orally as a "hands up" survey. Some suggested teams include:
- Youngest in the family
- Oldest in the family
- Have a pet/dog/cat/car
- Have been in hospital
- Have black hair
- Have green eyes
- Like basketball
- Have travelled overseas

Magic Mirror (for Kindergarten)

Tape a mirror on the bottom of a decorated lidded box. Discuss with the children the fact that the box has inside it a clue to the most important person in the world. Ask them if they know who it might be? Take children outside individually to look inside the box and see themselves. Ask each child to keep the identity of the person in the box a secret until everyone has seen it. Explain in a discussion afterwards that the box is special because it shows that each person is special.

Success story

At the end of the day, ask students to share something they learned, or achieved that day. Stress that it doesn't have to be about schoolwork: it could be something helpful they did in the playground, or at home, as long as it is something they are proud of.

Adding Adjectives

Add a positive alliterative adjective to your students' names; for example, Jolly Joel, Clever Katie, Strong Stephen, Amazing Amanda.

Activities adaptable for all grades

Many of the following activities can be adapted for older students in subject specific classrooms, or can be used with your roll-class or support group if those systems operate in your school.

Comments Box

Have a box in which students can write notes to you as the teacher. Make it the rule that any sort of comment can be made, so students will not be harassed if they are observed posting a note. This will give students an opportunity to let you know privately if they have a problem at school, such as being bullied.

Develop class profiles

Have all students write a one paragraph description of themselves and combine into a class profile. If you have the technology, develop a class web page.

Welcome Kit (a good activity for support groups)

Develop a small welcome package for new students. Include the class profile, a map of the school, information about school clubs and activities, a copy of the class rules or expectations and perhaps even a snack bar. If you have advance notice that the student will be arriving, make a welcome banner to greet the student when he enters.

Make class posters

Discuss statements with your class that can be used as a type of class motto and make a poster that can be displayed prominently, perhaps on the classroom door or as a banner above the blackboard. It is important that everyone agrees on the statement and that it is a constant visual reminder of that agreement. Statements may include something like "We care – we share" for lower grades; or something like "We accept and value individual differences" for older students. Students can sign the poster to show that they agree with it.

Send cards to sick students

If a student is away with a significant illness, send a card from the class with individual messages from students. Students of all ages appreciate this, even if adolescents are less likely to admit it.

Joke Board

A notice board could be devoted to subject-related jokes or cartoons.

Naming strengths

Have students write their own name vertically and add positive adjectives for each letter; for example

Kind
Athletic
Tolerant
Inquisitive
Eager

Jovial
Amiable
Mighty
Energetic
Sympathetic

Student surveys

At the earliest opportunity, have the students complete a personal survey. Complete one yourself and make it available for the students. Present it as a fun activity, as an opportunity for you to get to know one another. Finding out as many of the students "favourite things" is important, and they are usually quite happy to write about these. This is also useful knowledge when determining rewards if incentive schemes are used in your classroom.

Surveys can be a non-threatening way to find out if bullying is occurring in your classroom. Excellent surveys for this purpose are available in Beane (1999). Questions will depend to some extent on the age group but you could include some of the suggestions in Box 2.3.

Box 2.3 Survey Questions

Name:
- Five words that your friends would use to describe you
- Favourite toy as a child (or now!)
- Favourite hobby
- Favourite TV show
- A person you admire
- Qualities you admire in adults
- Where you want to be in five, ten years from now
- What characteristic would you like to have more of?
- Your favourite possession
- Something you hope to learn this year
- Your favourite subject
- Your least favourite subject
- A special memory
- A funny thing you once did
- A favourite book/story
- A funny thing that has happened to you
- Your favourite movie
- If you had to be someone else apart from yourself, you would be ...
- Name something you hate to do. Why?
- Something nice you did for someone once
- Something you tried hard to do
- My biggest worry is ...
- If I were an animal I would like to be ...
- The best thing about this class is ...
- The worst thing about this class is ...
- I would like to be the world record holder in ...
- I wish adults would ...
- I wish adults wouldn't ...
- I would like my nickname to be ...

PART TWO

SETTING SAIL IN FAIR WEATHER

Chapter Three

Developing Classroom Rules and Routines

Introduction

Just as an understanding of how different each of your students may be is important, as is the need to be aware of how you can develop a positive emotional tone in your classroom, there are many organisational issues that need to be considered once you enter the classroom. There are specific strategies that assist the development of an effective learning environment and limit the opportunities for disruptive behaviour.

It is in everyone's interest for classroom activity to run smoothly. Good classroom management has been consistently associated with academic achievement and increased time-on-task (Bender & Mathes, 1995; Fuller, Miller, & Lesh, 1989; Gettinger, 1986; McDonnell et al, 1996; Palmer & Neal, 1994; Purvis et al, 1992; Wheldall & Carter, 1996; Yates, 1988; Yehle & Wambold, 1998). When students are on-task, they are not acting out or affecting the learning of others.

There are two major strands to classroom management:
- The Development of a Set of Rules or Code of Conduct
- The Development of Classroom Routines

The Importance of a Set of Rules or Code of Conduct

Negotiating just how the complex mix of individuals within any class is going to learn, even survive together, is an important part of establishing an environment which will limit problem behaviours. Rules exist in every social group, whether they are made explicit or not. People are more likely to obey rules if they have some input into them. Students are more likely to obey rules if they help to create them, but in most cases, they will still need the guidance of their teacher.

Place rules within a context of rights and responsibilities

Classroom rules should be placed within a context of mutual rights and responsibilities. A good place to start is a brainstorming session about what the students see as their rights (they'll be quite vocal and knowledgeable about this!) A discussion of the rights of the teacher should follow, incorporating such things as the right to teach, the right to respect, and the right to a safe environment. Clear parallels with the students' rights should emerge. A "Bill of Rights" for your class could be developed.

The discussion should incorporate the fact that in order to be able to take advantage of personal rights, we are dependent on others meeting their responsibilities. For example, in order for you to experience your right to speak, others must allow you to be heard. It is very important that this connection be made, as the link between the two are conveniently forgotten at times. Some examples of this are included in Figure 3.1 and 3.2.

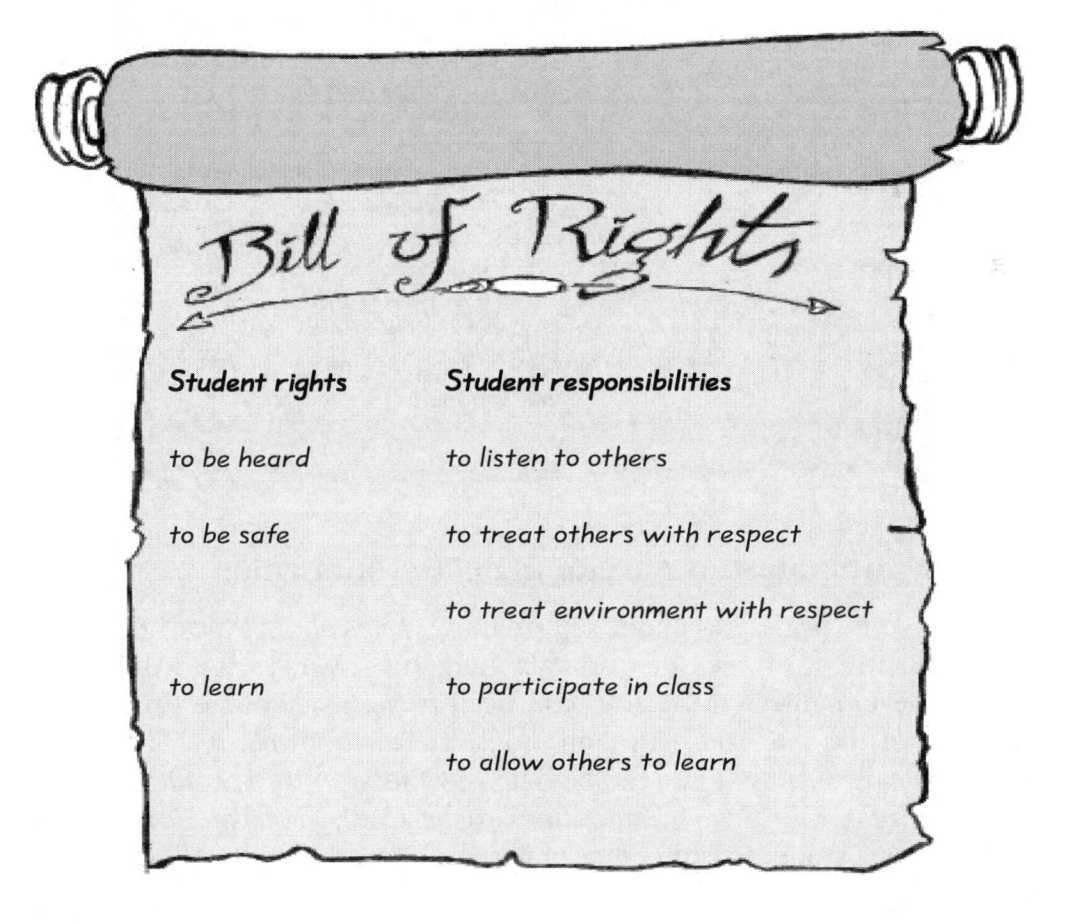

Figure 3.1 Students' Rights and Responsibilities

Bill of Rights

Student rights	Student responsibilities
to be heard	to listen to others
to be safe	to treat others with respect
	to treat environment with respect
to learn	to participate in class
	to allow others to learn

Figure 3.2 Teachers' Rights and Responsibilities

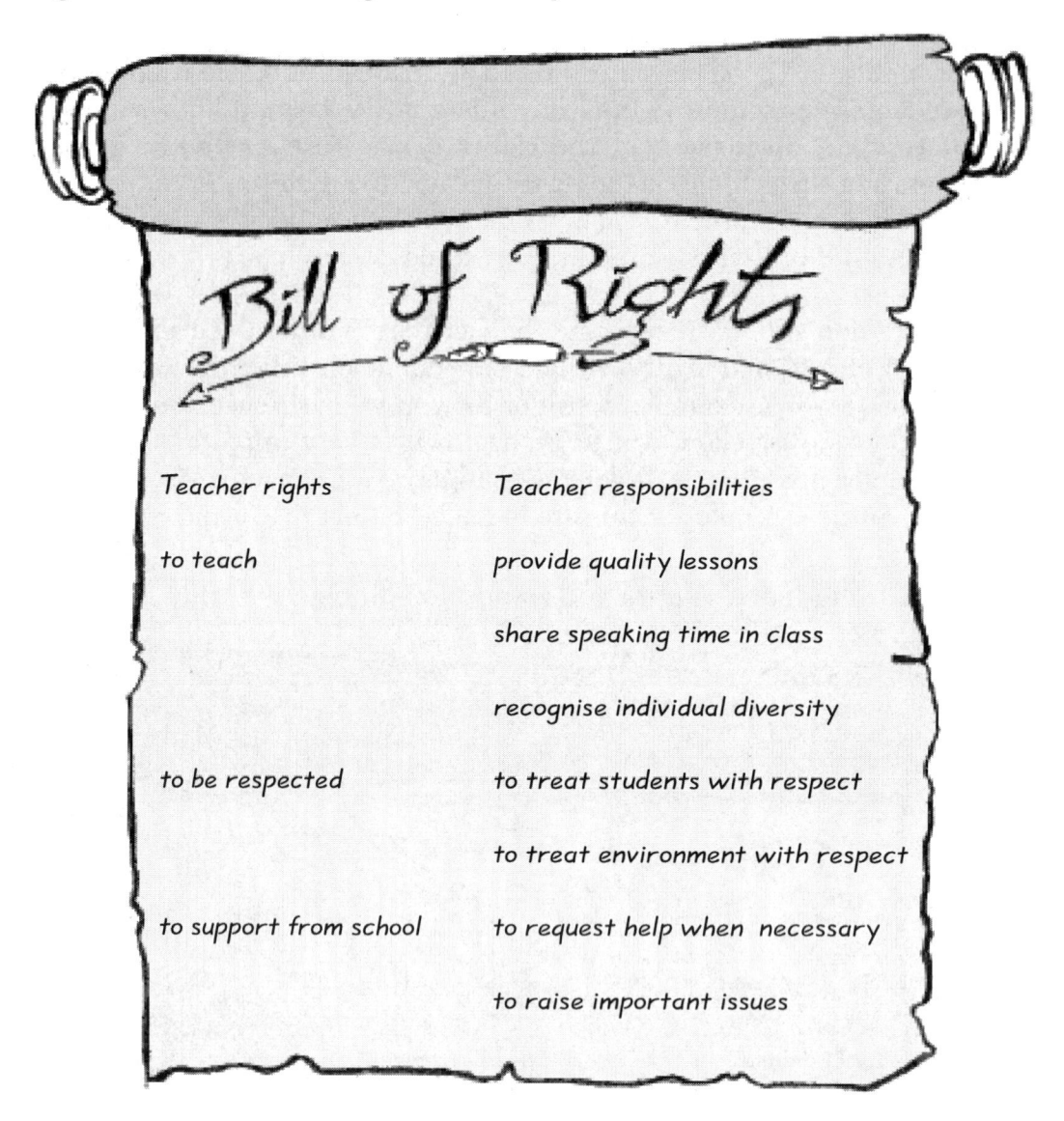

Bill of Rights

Teacher rights	Teacher responsibilities
to teach	provide quality lessons
	share speaking time in class
	recognise individual diversity
to be respected	to treat students with respect
	to treat environment with respect
to support from school	to request help when necessary
	to raise important issues

General principles for developing classroom rules

There are some principles about rule-making (rules about rules!) that help the establishment of a set of workable guidelines. We stress at this point that, whatever subject you teach, you need to set aside some time at the beginning of the year to set up and practise classroom rules. They don't have to be called *rules*. They can be listed as *Classroom Expectations, Our Class Contract, Our Agreement, Rules to be Cool, Code of Conduct*, or whatever your students can come up with.

Develop rules collaboratively

Most models of classroom management acknowledge the need for students themselves to be part of decision-making processes within a classroom. You are ultimately responsible for what occurs in your classroom and therefore you have the right of final decision-making, but there is nevertheless a great deal of room for student collaboration. Clearly, more productive discussions will occur with older students. With very young children, rules devised by you may be more appropriate, but these should be clearly explained to the students.

An important caveat

If the class is a particularly tough one, with a number of non-compliant students, or if a situation has developed whereby a greater degree of teacher control needs to be established, we believe you have the right – and the responsibility - to develop clear and explicit guidelines for behaviour without input from the class. These should then be discussed, and perhaps refined, with the class, but under your close guidance.

Make rules reasonable and enforceable

A rule of "No talking" is not reasonable in any classroom, although there may well be a rule about noise levels or when talking is permitted. The expectations should be achievable otherwise too much teaching time will be spent trying to enforce them.

Match to school policy

Any classroom rules you make must be consistent with the school policy. This is very important if you send a student from the classroom. There are strict guidelines relating to supervision of students and students are always expected to be under teacher supervision of some kind. The younger the child, the more direct the supervision required.

Make rules short and positive

Make the rules short and express them positively. There are a couple of reasons for not expressing rules in the negative. The first is that you are never going to be able to list *all* the things that are unacceptable in your classroom. A clever bush lawyer may come up with, "but the rules don't say I can't stab Christy with my pen". Another reason is that negatively expressed rules don't give direction as to what *should* be done. It is more useful to say, "Listen when other people are talking" rather than a general, "No talking".

Connect rules to consequences

Students should also be involved in developing consequences for rule infringement. This can require careful direction by the teacher, as some children, certainly in middle primary years, can come up with quite punitive consequences. (There's not really a place for stocks in the playground any more!) Class consequences should always be consistent with school-wide policies. Consequences should be part of an overall response rather than having specific consequences attached to specific "offences". There should also be a series of consequences of increasing severity to allow for the full range of behaviours that may occur. An example of this is seen in Box 3.1.

Box 3.1 Consequences should be associated with Rules

> OUR CLASS AGREEMENT
> **Our class has decided to:**
>   Raise hand to speak
>   Listen to the speaker
>   Take care of our classroom
>   Work and play safely and fairly
> **If we don't, we will:**
>   Write out our rules
>   Lose group points
>   Move to different table
>   Leave classroom

Have only a few

It is best to avoid a long list. Three to five class rules should suffice. This means, however, that they need to be general in nature and cover broad areas. You could have one rule covering talking, another for movement in the classroom, and one addressing how students should get attention. Safety issues in some senior classes also require a rule, particularly in science or practical subjects.

Teach and revise rules

For the first two weeks, read through the rules at the start of each day. Refer to them regularly and apply them consistently. It is critical that everyone in the class understands the rules, and what they mean in practice. If abstract terms like *respect* are used, they may require some discussion of practical examples. This is particularly important for students with learning difficulties who may have difficulty with abstract notions. It is often useful to revise or amend the class rules at certain times throughout the year. The beginning of each term or at the beginning of a new unit of work would be appropriate times, especially if new working arrangements are likely to occur, such as group work or additional visits to the library or computer laboratories.

Reinforce consistently

You need to reinforce the negotiated rules consistently, especially during the first few weeks of the year or your time will have been wasted. Each time a student infringes the code, reference should be made to the relevant rule.

Display rules prominently

In primary grades, the rules should be displayed prominently. Some teachers move them around the room regularly to avoid them becoming too much "part of the furniture". The rules could also be written on the inside cover of one of their regularly-used books.

The rules can also be written up as a type of contract which the teacher and students sign. They can be sent home for parent signatures to reinforce their importance. The point is that they are not developed and then forgotten or not referred to again. The students need to be very aware of what rules are governing behaviour in their classroom. No matter how carefully they may have been established, if they are not regularly referred to and followed, the effort will have been wasted.

At the senior secondary level, a discussion about the students' personal expectations of senior secondary school may begin the negotiation process. Classroom behaviours that will assist the achievement of those goals can then be discussed and formed into a set of Class Expectations, as in Box 3.2.

Box 3.2 Suggestion for Senior Classes

> **CLASS EXPECTATIONS**
>
> In order to achieve our goals this year, we need to be orderly, organised and on time; apply ourselves in class and at home; contribute our ideas honestly and listen to the contributions of others. We will do this in an environment of mutual respect and support for each other's needs, ideas, and aspirations.

The Importance of Establishing Routines

The use of specific routines for regular classroom activities has been consistently associated with increased time on task (Bender & Mathes, 1995; Fuller, Miller, & Lesh, 1989; Gettinger, 1986; McDonnell et al, 1996; Palmer & Neal, 1994; Pisarchick, 1989; Purvis et al, 1992; Wheldall & Carter, 1996; Yehle & Wambold, 1998). Good classroom managers establish routines for dealing with such things as organisation of materials and requests for help; they minimise interruptions; and they maintain efficient transitions.

Many daily interruptions to teaching time occur because workable routines are not in place in the classroom. Careful thought should go into how you organise your classroom so that minimum time is spent on organisational matters, on transitioning from one lesson to the next and on redirecting students back to their tasks. Breaks between lessons, and interruptions to lessons to find or organise equipment are precisely those times that students who are easily distracted or inclined to move off task, will do so.

We also believe you have the right to limit the number of interruptions you experience through requests from other teachers for equipment, messages about lost clothing or equipment, or communications from the office. If interruptions of this nature are interfering with your teaching, add this to the agenda at a staff meeting. Schools are responsible for ensuring their communication systems facilitate your teaching, not hinder it.

Entry and exit procedures

Some teachers (and at least one of the authors was one of them early in her teaching career) operate on the assumption that students can read their mind. Students will not know that you want them to line up outside the door before entering if that is not explicitly explained, and then expected, of them. Explicitly tell them what they should do once they enter: put equipment away; get equipment out; sit on the mat at the front; or whatever. A general routine that is followed most days is useful, especially for students who are easily distracted.

You should also decide on the procedure when the end of the period in secondary school, or a recess or lunch break in primary school, is signalled. In some classrooms, the bell is followed by an immediate packing up and frantic lunge towards the door by all students. It is more appropriate to tell students that the bell is a signal to the teacher, and that students should wait for a teacher direction before packing up.

Gaining student attention

You need to have a strategy for gaining the students' attention. There are any number of ways to do this and we will provide some suggestions in Chapter Four. The point is, you need to teach the students *your* method, and practise and reinforce it many times during the early part of the year.

Gaining teacher attention

It's important that you explain to the students how they should get your attention. There may be a general procedure, such as students raising their hands to indicate they require help. For some lessons, there may be different procedures. They may write their name on the board if they need a conference during a writing session. Rarely does a teacher decide that the procedure should be that the students click their fingers loudly, call out the teacher's name or follow the teacher around until they are finally attended to, but this is often observed.

What to do when finished

If your students know what they can go on with when they have finished set work, and if it is motivating, there is less chance that they will find something distracting or disturbing to fill the void. Have a plan for the early finishers. If the same students are continually finishing early, and checks ensure that they have completed the work successfully, they may need an extended program. This then becomes a curriculum match issue. However, there is still a need to ensure that students know what to do if they finish early.

Collection and distribution of materials

Different systems work but *some* system is necessary. Colour-coded trays are a useful idea for books that are collected regularly. Group monitors may be used to distribute books and materials.

Participation in lessons

Different lesson types may require different participation procedures. Some seatwork is individual and should require no talking. Other work may be done in groups, in which case some level of talking will be necessary.

A useful strategy for these occasions is a noise metre. These metres indicate different levels of noise and the appropriate level is marked before the seatwork begins. You may have markers for "no talking", "partner voice", and "group talking". If the noise level rises, as it usually does over a period of time, the teacher adjusts the metre and indicates that it is unacceptable. A small bell can be used to draw students' attention to this. This can be used as warning before a consequence is applied.

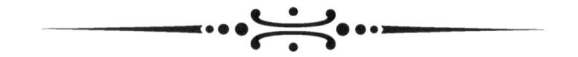

Some ideas to help you organise your routines

Late Log

If you find that students arriving late, even with legitimate reason, are becoming a distraction, put a "Late Log" close to the door. This should be divided into columns for the date, time, student's name and reason. Students need to sign in without interrupting the class or you, and then be seated and wait until you are able to attend to them. A Late Log can help identify patterns of behaviour that may help you and the student reduce lateness.

"Quick Starts"

Have written in a particular place on the board or on a separate easel, a few different activities that the students can do as soon as they arrive. Make them brief, able to be completed in about five minutes. This is a good place to practise recently learned skills but you could include a puzzle, code or fun activity occasionally. Students who complete them should get recognition or points in whatever system you are operating in the classroom to encourage them to settle down quickly.

Task sheets

Develop and laminate task sheets for regular classroom activities such as journal writing, creative writing, editing, setting up for art, setting up for an experiment, etc. Place these in appropriate areas so students become familiar with the routines, and can check if they are not sure what to do.

For fast finishers

Have a task sheet, such as that described above, which lists items that need to be checked when students believe they have finished. Also have a special FFF (Fast Finishers File) box which has in it activities that can be done by those who have completed their work and checked the task sheet. Some suggestions are included in Box 3.3.

Box 3.3 Fast Finisher Suggestions

- Write topics on a piece of paper for impromptu one-minute speeches to be placed in a designated box
- Write a note for the class post box
- Complete sentences/write a paragraph beginning:
  ~ Cars should be banned because…
  ~ If all roses were black…
  ~ Pills should replace food because
  ~ Artists are more important than economists because…
  ~ Economists are more important than artists because…
  ~ If there was no sun…
  ~ If it rained every day…etc.
- Make up a proverb
- Write a limerick
- What three items would you like to have with you if you were stranded on a desert island. Why?
- Write a message in code and include the code on a separate piece of paper.
- Write a letter to your local representative about an issue of concern in your community

Periodic "Sort and Save"

At the end of each week or perhaps each unit of work, have a "sort and save" activity where students go through their desks/folders and organise their work. This is a good opportunity for you to model how to sort out materials, file appropriately, decide what is no longer needed and organise folders. This prevents a collection of torn and crumpled papers, and other rubbish in desks or trays and keeps materials in order.

YOYO (You're on your own) time

Explain to your class that you need uninterrupted time sometimes when you are working with an individual or a small group of students. (Ensure that everyone gets the opportunity to receive your small group help at some time, and that it is not always the same group which receives your undivided attention.) Explain that on those occasions, the class will be expected to work on its own, hence the YOYO (You're on your own) sign.

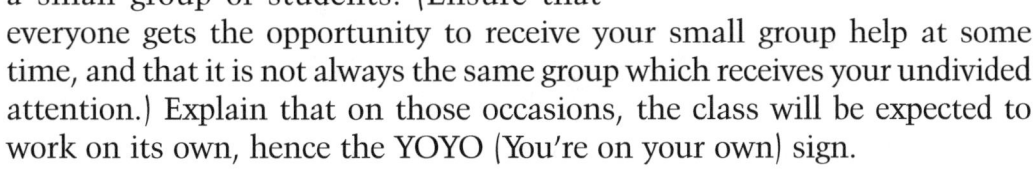

On these occasions, place close to where you are working, a YOYO sign on a poster next to a kitchen timer which shows how much time you need. Suggest some alternatives to requesting your help on the poster, such as

- check the task sheet
- ask a friend (quietly)
- work on something else

This, of course only works if the class has developed some level of self-management skills, but is a good training device to assist this development. Fifteen to twenty minutes is reasonable yoyo time in primary classrooms – longer than that would be difficult for most students.

A Final Note

The time spent establishing and practising routines is well worth the effort. At the start of each school year with new class(es), consider allocating 20 minutes per day for three or four days in the first week of the term to training the students in such things as class communication, transitions between activities, entering the classroom, distributing books, starting work, and so on. This will help you make the best use of classroom time throughout the entire year.

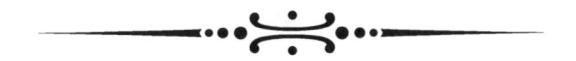

The Casual Teachers' Survival Guide

We're going to spend a little time here discussing strategies specifically for casual teachers. Many teachers begin their careers in this, undoubtedly the hardest, way. Unfortunately the experience for many is such that they leave the profession before ever having their own class. The reason most often quoted for leaving, is difficulty managing student behaviour.

Have a survival plan

It is even more important that casual teachers approach their day with the advantage of prior planning. Those schools that give you as much notice as possible will be rewarded with a better prepared teacher and a less disrupted day for the students. If you are able to arrive at the school with the time and the access to relevant staff or documents, there are more things you can do to ensure a productive day.

Check school policy

If possible, ask about the school policy on removal of students from class and such things as using sweets as rewards if you plan to do that. We are making no judgements about this – it is our belief that the judicious use of sweets (the only "performance enhancing drugs" we recommend!) is sometimes useful and justifiable.

Check on students with special needs

Some students may have medical conditions, such as diabetes or epilepsy, that you need to be aware of. Asking about these things also alerts school personnel that you are "on the ball". You should also ask if any students are on specific behaviour contracts, and particularly if they are in the class you will be teaching. Many casual teaching fiascos could have been averted if a casual teacher had been informed that they had a student with a particular problem in the class.

Getting initial attention

This is one of the most essential, and sometimes the hardest, skill to accomplish, especially for casual teachers who do not have the luxury of knowing students' names, and the normal classroom routines. This, of course, is then exploited by some students for whom "casual teacher baiting" is a favourite school sport.

Often an assertive but pleasant manner and clearly stated directions will suffice. If you find that the class is very noisy on entry, and barely a head turns towards you, move around the class and speak to individuals, introducing yourself and asking for the names of some key individuals. It is important to get to know the names of the "hard core" students as quickly as possible.

Another strategy is to write the plan for the lesson or the session on the board. Include - and this is critical - a reward or surprise component at some point. Don't be too explicit about it. Just write SURPRISE! or MYSTERY ACTIVITY or simply a large question mark at some point (usually the end) of the lesson or session In this way students are immediately aware that it may just be worth their while to pay attention. This also works if you have been in the room for several minutes and have been unable to get the attention of the whole class. In our experience, this nearly always results in someone asking what this will be – it only takes one student to notice. Explain that this will be a surprise activity which will occur when you have finished what you need to do for that lesson.

You could distribute small pieces of cardboard which can be folded to form name cards to be placed on the front of their desks. Primary-aged children are usually quite happy to record their names and decorate their own name cards as an initial activity.

Another activity which usually works successfully with students up to about Grade 9 is a multi-level worksheet which can be completed by individuals. Distribute the sheets quickly when you enter and explain that there will be small mystery prizes for the winning entries. Students will usually write the correct name on the sheet if there is a prize attached! As students complete the activity, remind them to write their name on the top of the sheet so you know who should receive the prizes. Circulate and consciously try to remember the names of the students whose voices were the loudest when you entered! Collect the sheets and mark at the first available opportunity – usually recess, unfortunately. Have prizes in different categories so many of the students will have a chance to win. In the worksheet shown as Box 3.4, there could be a prize for the longest word, the most unusual word, the most five letter words, etc. This ensures that more of the students will take the activity seriously. Remember, students who normally do not do well in class are those who will usually cause the most trouble, especially for a casual teacher.

Box 3.4 Multi-level Worksheet

NAME:
How many words can you make from the letters in
UNDERSTANDING

(only use each letter as often as it occurs in "understanding")

2 letters	3 letters	4 letters	5 letters	more than 5 letters

Use a seating plan

It is often worth using a seating plan. Ask one of the more sensible students (this is usually easy to determine quite early in the day) if he or she could draw one for you. This may not be possible on a single day, but if you have been given a block of several days or longer, and the class is difficult, it is certainly worthwhile isolating the more difficult students in strategic positions rather than allowing three or four difficult students to sit together and play off each other.

Establish the timetable for the day

Even if you have not used a written timetable to get the attention of the class, a timetable for the day written up on the board demonstrates to the class that you are well prepared and have a plan. This may merely reflect the usual timetable, in which case it shows that you know what goes on.

Build in class reward/mystery element

Even if you are merely following the regular timetable, you could still include a mystery or surprise activity to keep the class motivated. Place it strategically towards the end of the session or day. Rewards could include a special game or listening to a CD.

Include group rewards

Many classrooms operate some sort of reward system. Sometimes it is more straightforward to use your own for the period that you are there. This often avoids the bush lawyers among the students from claiming some inequity in the implementation of the regular system.

Establish expectations

It is usually not possible to have a collaborative discussion about class rules for the day, but a few minutes spent establishing your expectations, with the use of your portable *Respect* chart (see next section), is time well spent.

Get to work (if in doubt, use your own and leave marked)

It's important to get to work quite quickly. Academic engagement prevents a great deal of off-task behaviour. Develop a supply of relevant activities for each grade level. If you don't understand what has been left by the teacher, use your own supplies. Try to make them more than time-fillers.

Leave relevant notes for teacher

As far as possible, mark any work done by the students throughout the day. This will be greatly appreciated by the returning teacher (and should alone guarantee a return call to the school). Also leave relevant notes for the teacher about anything significant that happened throughout the day.

Concluding the Day

Always try to finish the day on a positive note. There should be some positive message about a student, group of students, or an incident that occurred throughout the day.

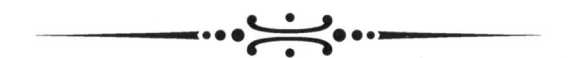

The Casual Teachers' Survival Pack

Extra class activities (if in doubt, do yours)

Hopefully, the regular class teacher will have left class work for you to do. Nevertheless, it is always wise to take extra activities with you that are relevant for the particular grade you are teaching. It may be that nothing has been left because the teacher had no warning of her absence. You may simply not understand the class program (sad but true) or exactly what was required. It is better that the students are actively engaged in activities that you understand. Try to make the planned activities legitimate for that grade level, rather than simply time-fillers. But do include some fun activity to use as a reward for a hard day's work.

Transition games/activities

For primary grades, take ideas for transition activities. A tables quiz, general knowledge quiz (*Sale of the Century* style), spelling bee, etc can be adapted for any grade. Inexpensive pencils, rulers, and so on make good prizes.

Reward ideas/system

Before you set out, have an idea of how you will motivate a class that may be restless and unsettled because the routine has been disrupted. Some younger classes respond to the simple appearance of a large, brightly-coloured box decorated with a large question mark on the outside. This can be the start to any sort of lesson – the anticipation of what's inside focuses the attention.

You may have a large clear jar into which you place marbles at regular intervals when students are on task, or when they come to attention quickly. When a predetermined number of marbles has been collected, there is a class reward such as choice of music to listen to, free time, a video, etc.

Raffle tickets also have a multitude of uses, with either individual students or teams. Students are rewarded with one half of a raffle ticket every time they are on task. At the end of the day or session, students can use the raffle tickets to "bid for" selected items or preferred activities. Of course, the more raffle tickets that they have collected, the better.

The raffle tickets stubs can also be placed inside a container and tickets can be drawn for prizes. Once again, the more tickets, the greater the chance of a prize.

Spare pens, pencils, etc

It is always worthwhile having spare pens and pencils to avoid the inevitable time-wasting that occurs when students suddenly realise they do not have the necessary equipment. Remember to retrieve these at the end of the period or the day. Although it is true that it is not your responsibility to supply students with these items, you'll save time, energy and frustration if you are able to (and such items are tax deductible).

Small notebook for follow-up

As a casual teacher, you will probably be tested more than the regular teachers. For your own credibility, it is a good idea to carry with you a small notebook so you can follow up students who misbehave, particularly when on playground duty. Even the act of recording something often limits the excessive behaviour as students realise that you are taking the situation seriously.

Plastic bags or envelopes

A few envelopes or plastic bags (sandwich size ziplock bags are highly recommended) are very useful to organise the various bits and pieces that assail a teacher during the first few minutes of a day. Some schools no longer have teachers collecting money for excursions, and so on, but many still do. There are inevitably absentee notes, lunch orders, messages and any amount of other organisational paraphernalia that needs organising within the first few minutes. A system of envelopes or plastic bags usually helps avoid a pile of unidentified bits and pieces by the end of the day.

Rules chart and noise meter

Many classrooms, if not all, will have class rules displayed. Unfortunately you will probably not know if they are in the classroom where you will be spending the day, nor if they are a set of rules that you can live with.

As a back-up for primary classes, take with you your own simplified rules chart. This can be as simple as a large "**R**" centred on a piece of cardboard and laminated. This stands for the quintessential classroom rule – RESPECT. Explain to the class that the **R** is to remind them that they should respect the teacher, each other and each other's property. This should cover most of what goes on in the classroom. Of course arriving with this means that there cannot be a great deal of collaboration about this rule, but you should be able to spend a few minutes at the beginning of the day explaining and discussing this.

In secondary classrooms, you can probably do without the visual reminder. A reference to your "one simple rule" and a brief discussion of respecting each other being your "modus operandi" will usually suffice in many secondary classes.

The noise metre mentioned earlier is also useful in primary classes.

Chapter Four

MANAGING BEHAVIOUR THROUGH EFFECTIVE TEACHING: THEORY AND PRACTICE

Introduction

The link between effective teaching and classroom management is strong. While even a highly experienced and motivating teacher can still have management difficulties, and some students test even the most patient and encouraging teacher, one of the most effective ways that you can avoid behaviour problems disrupting your class, is to keep the students busy working. When students are busy working, they are not talking inappropriately, running around the room, being rude or interfering with other students.

Time on Task and Academic Engaged Time

We referred briefly in the last chapter to students being on task and academically engaged. When students are doing what they should be doing, whether it be reading, listening to instructions, completing maths algorithms, or even clearing up after an activity or lining up, they are referred to as being *on task*. That is, on-task behaviour means anything that the teacher has directed them to do, whether it be of an academic nature or not. The more time on task, the less disruptive behaviour. The two cannot exist together!

If students are actually doing some academic task like oral reading, writing an essay, conducting an experiment, taking notes from a text, they are referred to as being *academically engaged*. Academic engagement is therefore a subset of time on task. Academic engagement refers to involvement in activity that is relevant, motivating and at the appropriate level of difficulty - not so easy that it becomes monotonous, nor so difficult that it causes frustration.

A further subset of academic engaged time is the time that the students are experiencing *high success rates in their learning*; that is, they are not simply doing "busy work" they are learning something. This is referred to as *academic learning time*. This is what you should aim for – high rates of academic learning time in your classrooms. You will then have the best situation possible: an organised, disruption-free classroom in which students are actively learning.

What are the best ways to do this? Do some teaching techniques work better than others?

What does the research say?

During the late seventies and eighties, a great deal of classroom-based research took place, investigating what teaching strategies kept students busily engaged in learning activity. This has been confirmed by many recent studies, including an extensive classroom-based study conducted by one of the authors of students with ADHD (Konza, 1999). The research has found that certain teaching procedures and practices are consistently associated with increased academic engagement and increased learning in academic subjects.

Now we could have an extensive debate here about the real purpose of schools and teaching. Is our aim just to develop the academic skill levels of our students? Most of us would answer an emphatic "No!" We want our students to learn social and interpersonal skills; to develop into caring and productive citizens who can resolve differences in democratic and non-violent ways; to approach life's problems in creative and divergent ways – that is, we want them to be more than good learners.

Nevertheless, we contend that developing the academic skills of our students can contribute to all of these attributes. Literacy and numeracy, a good general knowledge, an understanding of the way the natural world operates, and so on are essential life skills. Success in basic academic areas enhances self esteem and prepares students for higher learning. Students who cause disruption in classrooms are often those who struggle in these basic areas: indeed the connection between learning problems and disruptive behaviour has been well established. Therefore, we believe that the effective teaching literature has a great deal to contribute to our understanding of how to manage behaviour while at the same time developing essential skills and increasing academic learning. This in turn leads to the development of other desirable outcomes of the school years.

We will discuss first the general findings of the effective teaching literature. These are often referred to as the "principles of effective teaching": principles which have been consistently found to be related to high levels of academic engaged time and higher academic achievement. We will then discuss how these principles might translate into classroom practice.

The Principles of Effective Teaching

1. The development of rules and routines

Good classroom management has been consistently associated with academic achievement and increased time-on-task (Bender & Mathes, 1995; Englert, 1984; Fuller, Miller, & Lesh, 1989; Gettinger, 1986; McDonnell et al, 1996; Palmer & Neal, 1994; Yehle & Wambold, 1998). Teachers who communicate rules and expectations regarding desired behaviours, particularly those that facilitate attention to task, have more successful students. That is why we began this part of the book with a discussion of how to establish rules and develop routines. They are the first step in developing a learning environment that reduces the chance of disruption. Rules and routines reduce transition time and eliminate inactive waiting time. Students are then less likely to become distracted, talk to their peers about unrelated matters, or engage in inappropriate activity.

There is likely to be quite a bit of noise and the opportunity for considerable time-wasting at the beginning of a lesson unless you have established a specific routine and taught the students to follow it. It is at this point that you can check that students have the required equipment, that any material that needs to be distributed is ready and that when the lesson proper begins, there is nothing that will distract attention.

With older students, teachers may begin with a quick quiz, or brief activity (see "Quick Starts", in Chapter 3) for which group points are awarded. Students can participate in these only if they are ready. (If it eventuates later that they were not ready, those points will unfortunately have to be deducted.) This settles the class, focuses attention and sets the right mood for the day.

If student workbooks need to be returned, it is usually a good idea to have a designated person (one from each group or row of desks) hand these out before any instruction begins. Students can write date, rule margins and be ready for action as soon as necessary. It will also be clear at this point who doesn't have a pen, pencil or ruler and this can be sorted out before any teaching begins.

Addressing these organisational matters before teaching begins is particularly important for students with attention problems. If there is a gap of several minutes between your demonstration or explanation, and the students starting to do the work alone, it is highly likely that they will have forgotten some important aspects of the demonstration. They need to be able to practise immediately before other matters, like looking for books or sharpening pencils, interfere.

2. Highly structured, teacher-directed teaching

More highly structured, teacher-directed instruction is consistently evident in classrooms where there are high levels of academic engagement and achievement (Askew, 1993; Bender & Mathes, 1995; Christenson et al, 1987; Gettinger, 1986; Hudson, 1997; Mathes & Fuchs, 1994). This does not necessarily mean that the classroom is not student-centred, but rather that it is the teacher who directs most learning activity in response to identified student needs. Teachers need to be in control of movement around the class, of what is being done and how it is being done. The use of whole class demonstrations, simple sequential directions, clear modelling of tasks, and specific and relevant feedback are features of this teacher-directed style.

Student freedom of movement, student task choice and a greater openness in the classroom is still often perceived as more desirable than a teacher-directed classroom (Hempenstall, 1996; Westwood, 1993). This, however, does not transfer in most classrooms into high levels of learning. Students who cause problems in classes are generally those who do not have the level of self-management that this sort of learning environment demands. An open classroom in which great student freedom of movement and task choice is the norm could lead to increased difficulties for students who find it difficult to focus and attend to task.

It makes sense that if students are free to move around whenever and wherever they wish and select their own activity that there will be more opportunities to talk to each other about unrelated matters, and to move off task in other ways. If you are having trouble in the classroom, it may mean that a more formal learning environment would provide the structure and the support that the students need to attend to their work and complete it.

Box 4.1 Explicit Teaching

> Effective teachers are more likely to say to the class, "Watch carefully, and listen to what I say to myself as I do this", rather than saying "See if you can work out how to do this for yourself" – often an invitation to failure for the lower ability students. They then provide carefully guided practice and corrective feedback to the students as they acquire the skill. This explicit teaching of task-approach strategies actually helps the students to become better "self-regulated learners", able to monitor their own performance and self-correct when necessary. (Westwood, 1993, p.24)

3. *An interactive teaching style*

The use of an interactive instructional style by the teacher increases academic engaged time (Allinder, 1994; Cannon et al, 1992; Christenson et al, 1987; McDonnell et al, 1996; Wheldall & Carter, 1996; Yehle & Wambold, 1998). If students believe they may be asked a question at any time, or that they can ask a question at any time, or that they may be asked to come out and do something on the board, or have a quick discussion about a point being made, they are far more likely to pay attention to what is being said. Students who feel accountable pay more attention and involve themselves more.

So, even though we have said that effective classrooms are more likely to be teacher-directed, this does not mean that you should be doing all the talking, but rather that you should provide opportunities for your students to interact and respond within demonstrations, explanations and so on. Your students need to be actively engaged in the task: talking, asking and answering questions, and discussing, rather than simply listening or observing.

Students with Asperger's Syndrome and ADHD may need to move more often than their peers. Including tasks that require active responding and providing opportunities for legitimate movement are useful in assisting these students remain on task. Arranging this as part of the class routine allows their movement to be less disruptive.

4. An academic focus

An *academic focus* refers to a task-oriented, purposeful, focused atmosphere in the classroom. Tasks are challenging, not simply time-fillers. It means that you must have a good grasp of the curriculum and of what has to be achieved for students to master the material; that you have planned lessons carefully; that you understand the specific objectives or outcomes you want from each lesson; and have planned assessments so that you can determine whether those outcomes have been achieved. When this level of planning takes place, your students will remain more on task, engage in less disruptive behaviour and learn more (Dunlap et al, 1982; Rosenshine & Stevens, 1986; Yates, 1988). Students generally feel satisfied when they are achieving, and so are less likely to become disruptive.

An academic focus doesn't mean that there is no enjoyment in class activity, nor that there is no warmth in the teaching/learning relationship. It doesn't mean that there is no time for the odd game, light-hearted moment or "feel–good" activity. In fact, these are often excellent ways to transition, or move between lessons quickly with little time lost. But it does mean that classroom activity has a sense of energy, achievement and purpose about it, rather than a series of low-demand, busy-work type activities that are neither satisfying nor productive. It also means that the students know that their work "counts" – that it will be marked. Students engage far more in tasks from which they will get feedback. If you continually leave student work unmarked, or delay returning material for lengthy periods, your students will be less inclined to do it. You have a great deal of control over this aspect of effective teaching.

5. Match between tasks and student interest and ability level

A close match between curriculum tasks and the ability of the students is essential in keeping students engaged in classroom activity (Christenson et al, 1987; Ellis, Worthington, & Larkin, 1994; Hudson, 1997; Reid, Maag, & Vasa, 1993; Scruggs & Mastropieri, 1992). Although matching tasks to the interests and ability levels of your students is, at first glance, a straightforward notion, it incorporates a combination of elements. It means that you must have a clear understanding of your students' abilities and interests in setting tasks. It demands that your students have the knowledge and skills to complete the task. It demands that necessary resources are available. It also demands that the student is motivated to complete the task. In a recent study, student task match was one of the two factors that was *always* present when students were on task more than 70% of the time (Konza, 1999).

Tasks which are below the ability level of students may fail to engage them just as tasks which are beyond their ability level may have a similar effect. Selecting appropriate tasks for your students is a major responsibility in order to ensure their involvement. It reduces time spent waiting for assistance or the use of off-task behaviour as an avoidance strategy. It also ensures relevance and high success rate, particularly when students are engaged in seatwork. Organised and structured guidelines and clear expectations, even of tasks such as discussions, will enable students to stay on task for longer periods.

This component of effective teaching also means that if you decide to use co-operative groups, or paired tasks, or research activities, that the students have the requisite skills to carry them out. You will probably have to teach these skills to your students over a period of time before using them. An important part of determining what teaching/learning activities you will use to teach specific material relates to ensuring that students have the necessary social, physical and academic skills to complete them successfully.

What you actually teach in the classroom can have a profound effect on the attitudes towards learning, and on the behaviour, of your students. You can help develop positive attitudes towards learning and the skills to continue learning throughout their lives. Through the material that you teach, and the way that you teach it, you can motivate, stimulate, and occasionally even enthrall your students as they learn. Students who are actively and enthusiastically involved in classroom learning are not likely to be disruptive.

Therefore careful planning of your classroom curriculum is highly likely to reduce disruption.

6. Close monitoring and supervision

If you supervise and monitor closely when your students are at their desks working independently or in groups they will remain on task and learn more (Bradley, Bjorlykke, Mann, Homon, & Lindsay, 1993; Carmichael et al, 1997; Crocker, 1986; Gettinger, 1986). Moving around the room allows you to identify students who are having difficulty, who are chatting about the weekend, who are painting their nails under the desk or reading the latest *Cosmo* or football magazine. Many time-wasting incidents can be addressed before they become a major problem. If your students know that you will be "on the prowl", they are less likely to attempt these activities anyhow.

Tempting as it might be, this is not the time to mark yesterday's creative writing/essays/tests/reports. This is the time to monitor what the students are doing now. Now is the best opportunity you have to see how the students are managing the material, where they are going wrong, or how quickly they have picked up the new information. If marking is left to out-of-class time, you don't have the opportunity to ask the student, there and then, to "work through this while I watch so I can see what you are doing". Trying to determine the thought processes of a student who has produced some perplexing answer to quite straightforward (you thought!) material can be a frustrating and time-consuming business. Monitoring while students are actually doing the work gives you the opportunity to watch the students handle the material independently, and you can learn a great deal of useful information in this way.

If you take your marking pen with you (and any stamps or stickers that you may be using in the younger grades), you should mark and sign any books you look at. This decreases marking you have to do outside class time, and generally ensures that you see the books more often, which parents respond to very positively.

This brings up the matter of the sort of material that should be given to students to do independently. Independent work should only be assigned when students have a high degree of success with the task. It is often simply because students are unable to manage the task that they begin to talk or engage in disruptive behaviour.

This also applies to homework. Asking students to "finish it off for homework" if they were not able to finish it during class is usually an unreasonable request. The students who could manage the work with no problems have generally completed the work in class. It is the students who couldn't do the work who are "dragging the chain". If they are unable to do it in class, there is even less likelihood that they will be able to do it at home. Homework of this nature is one of the greatest causes of tension in homes and adds considerably to negative feelings about school, teachers and learning on the part of many students and their parents. Teaching is your job, not the parents. It doesn't become their responsibility because you ran out of time or because you weren't able to teach it successfully. This is akin to parents sending the ironing to school for you to do because they didn't have enough time to get it done! Think carefully about how, what and why you set homework!

There is also evidence that increased on-task activity occurs if you move to the students requiring the assistance, rather than have them come to you. If you remain at your desk, and have students come out to you, it doesn't take long before a line of waiting students begin to obscure your view of what is going on in the room, at which point more and more students move off task.

Students with ADHD need to be monitored particularly closely because of their predisposition to move off task which is part of the ADHD condition. Seating them close to the front, but to one side is usually a good position (but not opposite doors or near high traffic areas). This allows you to move to them quickly but also places the student out of the direct line of vision of most of the rest of the class. A quick, "Back to work" as you fly past is not enough for these students. It is important to wait with the student or maintain visual contact until he has started to follow your directions.

Monitoring and supervision are essential even when students are working on group tasks. Group work demands many skills that the disruptive students in your class are unlikely to have. They may be taught these skills over a period of time, but an initial group activity is not the time to nip off to the equipment room to photocopy some worksheets, to organise materials for later, or mark previous work.

7. *A brisk pace*

Maintaining the momentum of a lesson is one of the most important, and perhaps one of the most difficult, aspects of effective teaching (Dunlap et al, 1982; Kounin, 1977; Rosenshine & Stevens, 1986). In the study done by one of the authors (Konza, 1999), maintaining the momentum of a lesson was the second factor that was *always* present when students were on task more than 70% of the time. You need to avoid spending too long on, or moving too quickly through, the material you are trying to teach. A brisk pace helps prevent student boredom, assists in keeping students on task, and so increases work output.

Students with ADHD become bored easily. It is even more important for these students to keep class activity moving at a brisk pace. Students with Asperger's Syndrome need momentum to keep them engaged rather than giving them the opportunity to retreat into their obsessional activity. Oppositional students who may be on special behaviour contracts or reward systems have the opportunity to score many points while they are busily engaged, which both encourages them and gives them vital practice in remaining on task.

8. *Immediate corrective feedback (mark often)*

An important principle of effective teaching relates to providing feedback very quickly so your students know how they are progressing (Christenson et al, 1987; Gettinger, 1986; Thurlow, Ysseldyke, & Wotruba, 1988). Signs of progress are very important motivators for students, especially those who find learning difficult. Providing immediate corrective feedback on both behaviour and academic work helps them remain on task. This provides the necessary direction and prevents them practising incorrect procedures, in addition to providing reinforcement for correct work, because an engaged class is one with few management difficulties.

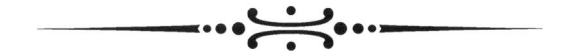

Putting it into Practice

We will now put these principles into practice, showing how the research discussed in this chapter can be translated into your everyday teaching. In this way you can, by a proactive approach to teaching, reduce the chance that students will move off task or become disruptive.

We are assuming that other points made earlier in this book have been addressed: that is, that you investigated the background experiences and abilities of your students; that you have thought carefully about how you can organise the classroom to promote a positive and supportive learning environment; and that you have developed rules and organisational routines with your class.

Be Prepared

- Check equipment
- Date on board
- Reminders on board
- Work assignments on board
- Timetable for day or lesson
- "Quick Start" activity on board

Student Entry

- Greet students personally as they enter
- Supervise morning routine (notes, money, lunch orders, etc)

Set up for instruction

- ➤ Students check that they have required equipment
- ➤ Books/equipment distributed by monitors
- ➤ Students prepare books if necessary (rule margins, write date, etc)

Establish attention

- ➤ Maintain pleasant but assertive manner (some students smell fear!)
- ➤ Ensure posture is upright
- ➤ Look confident and in control

For K-2

- ➤ Repeat simple clapping rhythm for children to copy until all are paying attention *or*
- ➤ Use word or phrase like "Freeze" or "Eyes to me" *or*
- ➤ Ring a tiny bell *or*
- ➤ Play a few chimes

For Grades 3-9

- ➤ Try to gain eye contact with a few students
- ➤ Say something like "Is everyone ready?", "settle down now" or "eyes to me"
- ➤ Scan room briefly to ensure that all students are attending
- ➤ Thank and/or reward those that are co-operating
- ➤ If someone isn't paying attention, mention their name
- ➤ When they look at you, smile and nod in recognition before you proceed

Use focus activity if necessary (see Box 4.2 for Turtle activity)

Box 4.2 Turtle

> ➢ Often when children return from the playground, especially if it's windy, they are not really ready to focus their attention on a lesson. When you notice that the children are very excitable, use the "turtle" technique.
>
> When the children are seated at their desks, talk about how a turtle goes into his shell to be calm. Ask them to put their forearms on their desks, cross them and put their heads down on their arms with their faces down. Tell them to imagine this is like a turtle drawing himself into his shell. In the shell, the turtle can be calm even though outside it's windy and noisy. Ask them to close their eyes and imagine the quietness and calmness inside their shells. Ask them to take six deep breaths and breathe out slowly. Finally ask them to imagine the sun setting and the evening sky getting darker – wait a minute and then ask them to imagine that dawn is coming, that it's gradually getting lighter. They are now calm and relaxed ready to start the new day (and the lesson).

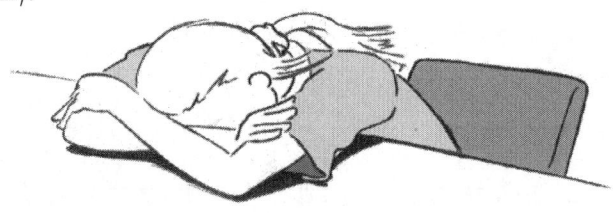

Review past work

> ➢ Link new lesson to previously learned material *or*
> ➢ Link to something students know *or*
> ➢ Show how information is important and/or relevant.

State the goals of the lesson clearly to the students

- Saying something like, "Today we are going to learn how to …"
- If this will form part of an assessment or portfolio, mention that also

Provide an outline of the lesson

- "First we're going to…, then…."

Demonstrate the new material or set the task

- Use small, sequential steps
- Incorporate many examples
- Check frequently for student understanding
- Use students' names frequently, especially those whose attention is likely to wander easily
- Ask a large number of simple questions which focus on the core content or activity
- Use visual aids and cues until students are confident and accurate in their responses
- Highlight key concepts by underlining or boxing, etc
- Use direct and explicit language

Provide further guided practice

- Students do examples on board or together
- Prompt and cue as necessary
- Provide worked example or sample of finished product if possible

Students move to independent practice or group activity

- Students work on set tasks
- Tell students how long they have for completion
- Monitor as students do independent or group work
- Take marking pen and stamps/stickers
- Assist those individuals who require it
- Mark as you circulate if students are doing independent work
- Spend maximum of 30-60 seconds with individuals

> If several students have similar problems, take them as a small group and work through the examples with them again

> If many students require your assistance, or are making too many errors, your demonstration or task-setting was probably not clear enough. In this case, you may need to reteach the material to the whole class.

Consolidate and review lesson content before closing

> At end of the lesson, review the main points of the lesson

> If setting homework, ensure students can do it independently

Provide regular revision and application throughout the following weeks

> Review main points at beginning of next lesson if the lesson involved a new skill.

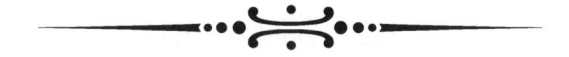

Additional strategies for more demanding students

Some of your students, especially those who are easily distracted, or harder to manage for other reasons, may need additional considerations throughout your teaching periods. The following strategies are useful for students who find it harder to remain on task (Jarman, 1996; Prior, 1996). We have also highlighted specific skills at the end of this section which you may need to teach quite explicitly to the students with greater self-management difficulties

Increase visual component of lessons

> Use more visual aids
> Point more
> Move more

- Add colour where possible
- Hold up materials you are referring to
- Use coloured worksheets

Use higher levels of positive reinforcement

- Use token reinforcement systems to reward students for staying on task and for work completion (see Chapter 6)

Chart Progress

- Use a graph to chart each student's progress towards an individual behavioural or academic goal
- Display individual graphs or place in individual workbooks. All class members should not be on the same chart. The point is for the individual student to see the progress he is making, not for class-wide comparisons to be made

Give short instructions and redirections

- Use simple rather than complex sentences

Reduce irrelevant stimulation

- Keep highly colourful classroom decorations/posters out of visual range of these students (i.e. at back of room rather than on front wall)
- Ensure there are no distractions hanging from ceiling
- Seat students near on-task peers
- Teach student to use blank sheet of paper to cover sections of page not being used
- Seat students away from high traffic areas

Divide work into smaller sections

- Mark and reward students as they complete each small section

Use visual time cues

- Use a kitchen timer or large clock face to remind students how much time they have to complete a set task

Add novelty to maintain attention to task

> Decorate worksheets
> Change format of response

Teach self-monitoring strategies

> Teach students to use buzzers or taped signals to remain on task (see Chapter Seven)

Assist with organisational strategies

> Designate student's space (eg, for younger students, put a masking tape **X** where they should sit on the mat)
> Model organisational skills (see "Sort and Save" in Chapter Three)
> Provide different coloured notebooks for different subjects
> Keep essential information and equipment in one place
> Number pages of handouts
> Use large simple fonts on worksheets
> Highlight critical information

Teach study skills

> For older students, specifically teach mnemonic strategies and outlining skills

Use computers

> Many programs provide continuous reinforcement, novelty, colour and movement, all of which appeal to distractible students. Ensure that you regularly provide opportunities for students to do similar tasks using pen and paper so skills are transferred and students don't become too dependent on computer technology.

Teach listening skills (for younger students)

> The 5 "L"s of listening (see Box 4.3)

Box 4.3 5 Ls of Listening

> **L**ook at the teacher
> **L**ips together
> Hands in **L**aps
> **L**egs and feet still
> **L**isten to what teacher says

Teach social skills (for younger students)

- Role plays
- Use of social stories
- Teach meaning of non-verbal cues
- Play social games like cards
- Use mirrors to teach about facial expression and body posture
- Teach conversational skills; how to maintain a topic; taking turns; how to interrupt
- Use videos with sound turned down to discuss facial expression, gesture, body movements, etc.

Limit use of figurative language

- When abstract terms must be used, explain them carefully

These strategies have been found to make staying on task easier. When students are on task, they learn more, and disrupt the class less. Your aim should be to have your students on task as much as possible to increase their learning outcomes, to decrease disruptive behaviour, and to make the teaching/learning process in your classroom a more enjoyable and productive experience for both you and your students.

Chapter Five

Existing Models of Behaviour Management

Introduction

We have looked at several different aspects of classroom management thus far. We have discussed individual differences, and our need to understand the ways in which students may differ and how these differences can affect their willingness and/or their ability to conform to acceptable classroom behaviour. These individual differences mean that you will need to develop a number of approaches, rather than just one approach, when dealing with students and student misbehaviour. If, as research has suggested (Fuchs, Fuchs, Fernstrom & Hohn, 1991; Kauffman, 1985) an individualised, flexible approach is warranted when examining problem behaviour, then it follows that intervention programs also need to be flexible and individualised.

We have also highlighted the importance of promoting a positive emotional climate in your classroom, and of developing rules and routines. In Chapter Four, we looked at the concepts of time-on-task and academic engaged time, and how maintaining high levels of each of these through effective teaching processes helps students remain on task and so disrupt class learning time less.

We now need to address those times when, despite all your planning, preparation, understanding and organising, you will need to redirect students back to task and assist the development of more appropriate behaviours in your students.

A number of educators, psychologists, psychiatrists and other people interested in children's behaviour have, over time, developed a range of responses to the problem of misbehaviour in the classroom and at school. Some responses have targeted the development of self-management skills in the students, whilst others have looked at teacher behaviours and the systems operating in schools.

Many of these models share common characteristics and draw inspiration from the same theoretical background. Others are more a collection of eclectic techniques. In order to place in context our own approach to managing low levels of disruption with classroom strategies (in Chapter Six) and more serious disruptive behaviours which demand additional out-of-class strategies (in Chapter Seven), we will present an overview of past and existing models of behaviour management.

Group Management Models

Group management models aim to develop teachers' skills in managing the different roles that teachers must play in the classroom. The role of the teacher in organizing the classroom environment and responding to difficult behaviour in a carefully planned and systematic way is emphasised in these models.

Lee and Marlene Canter's *Assertive Discipline*

Lee and Marlene Canter's (1976; 1990) Assertive Discipline model has as its basic premise that both teachers and students have needs which must be met in the classroom. Assertive teachers will not tolerate pupils stopping them from teaching or stopping other students learning. Most importantly, an assertive teacher will recognise and reinforce appropriate behaviour when it is displayed (Scherer, Gersch & Fry, 1990, p.154). The main focus of Canter and Canter's model is on teachers assertively insisting students behave properly, and on providing teachers with a well organised procedure for following through when this does not happen.

Key Concepts from the Assertive Discipline Model

- Ineffective teaching is directly related to inadequate classroom discipline;
- Firm control is not stifling and inhumane;
- Teachers have basic rights, including the right to establish the best teaching situations, to expect and request appropriate behaviour and the right to receive help when needed;
- Students have basic rights including a teacher who sets clear limits, and an awareness of the consequences of inappropriate behaviour;
- Both teachers' and students' rights are met through assertive discipline.

Canter and Canter indicated that if teachers are to become more assertive they need to clearly identify behaviour expectations, develop a willingness to let students know what they like and don't like, use a firm tone, maintain eye contact, use non verbal gestures, follow through with promised consequences and be assertive in confrontations with students.

Canter and Canter suggest four steps are needed for the implementation of assertive discipline:
- recognising and removing roadblocks to assertive discipline;
- practising the use of assertive response styles;
- learning to set limits;
- learning to follow through on limits and implementing a system of positive assertion.

Although assertive discipline programs can begin at anytime during the year, the beginning of the year (or when you are taking over the class for the first time) is the most appropriate time to begin. When the class is first brought together, rules (no more than five) should be discussed and recorded. Parents should be informed by letter of the classroom discipline code. These rules should be constantly referred to and reinforced by the teacher.

These consequences of breaking rules should be spelled out to the students so that the responsibility for their behaviour is with them. The teacher must be comfortable with the consequences and they must be presented in a calm manner. The consequences should be presented as the choice the student made by not adhering to the rules. Consequences should be implemented as soon as possible after the incident.

Canter and Canter also suggest using assertive skills with parents and principals. This means recognising your own need for help and assistance in dealing with a difficult child. The message here is "you are not alone unless you let yourself be so".

You can see that Canter and Canter's approach uses techniques from a range of sources. Their use of consequences is behavioural, but they also include aspects of a psychological needs model.

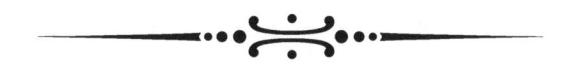

Fritz Redl

Redl developed a four-part approach to assist classroom teachers in dealing with inappropriate behaviour: permitting, tolerating, intervening and preventative planning (1972).

Key Concepts from the Redl Model

❖ *Permitting*

Although teachers often emphasize what students in their class *cannot* do, they are seldom clear enough about what they *can* do, that is, what constitutes acceptable behaviour. Redl suggested that teachers should let students know quite explicitly what behaviour is appropriate.

❖ *Tolerating*

Redl argued that sometimes unacceptable behaviour can be tolerated due to the circumstances surrounding it. He suggested a number of factors which need to be considered when deciding whether unacceptable behaviour may be tolerated:

- The developmental phase of the student (third graders who tell tales or sixth graders who giggle);
- Situational behaviour (some unusual behaviour may be precipitated by illness, divorce or death);
- Relationship building (sometimes unacceptable behaviour may be tolerated because the teacher is attempting to build a trusting and working relationship with the student);
- Wrong place wrong time (Redl suggested that, at particular times such as two minutes before final bell or in a public place, it might be better to accept certain behaviour and follow it up at a later time).

❖ *Intervening*

Some behaviours cannot be tolerated. In these situations, Redl suggests a series of intervening strategies including:

- Planned ignoring (some behaviour will disappear if left unchallenged);
- Signal interference (a cue to the student before they attempt the inappropriate behaviour may curb it);
- Proximity control (move near the misbehaving student to indicate control);
- Interest-boosting (help a student with new material to avoid any inappropriate behaviour);

- Hypodermic affection (an affectionate word or gesture may diffuse frustration);
- Tension decontamination through humour (humour can relieve the tension);
- Hurdle help (guide the student through the difficult aspects of the work);
- Restructuring (abandon an activity or lesson if it is not working);
- Direct appeal to value areas (appeal to the student's values);
- Removing seductive objects (remove objects that may be just too irresistible for students);
- Antiseptic bouncing (removing student from group for a few minutes may help).

❖ Preventative Planning

Redl argued that if children misbehave during certain times and/or in certain places then changes to class procedure might be necessary.

Frederic Jones

Frederic Jones, a psychologist, spent hundreds of hours in primary schools observing how teachers manage their classrooms. From his observations he identified a series of skills which he believed were critical for effective classroom management. He combined these in his *Classroom Management Training Program* (1987a; 1987b).

Jones determined that teachers in typical classrooms spend approximately 50% of their instructional time managing students who are off task and disturbing other class members. Most of the teacher's lost time is as a result of two kinds of inappropriate behaviour on the part of students: firstly, getting out of their seat and secondly, talking without permission.

Many effective techniques, while being instinctive to "natural" teachers, can be learned. When teachers are able to provide individual help to students quickly and effectively, the students are better behaved and complete more work. Most of these problems can be addressed through:
- the effective use of body language;
- use of incentives for motivation;
- providing efficient help for students during seatwork.

Key Concepts from the Jones Model

❖ Body Language

Teachers reveal interest, authority, confidence level and enthusiasm through body carriage. Jones' training program concentrates on helping teachers learn to use their physical mannerisms to set and enforce behaviour limits. These physical mannerisms include:

- posture, whereby authority is conveyed by the teacher's carriage;
- eye contact, whereby an effective teacher constantly looks around the room making eye contact with as many students as possible. This conveys the message that the teacher is aware of what is happening in the classroom;
- facial expressions which do much to communicate teacher's mood and can be used, via winks, smiles, raised eyebrows, etc, to convey humour, approval, disapproval and appreciation to the students. A teacher's sense of humour is greatly valued by students;
- gestures (palm out - stop; palm up wriggling fingers - continue; finger to lips - quiet; thumbs up - approval) which can be used without interrupting instructional time.

To use physical proximity effectively Jones argues that seats should be arranged in a semi-circle so that the teacher can quickly circulate around the classroom. Tone and strength of voice also convey messages and are far more useful than volume of voice.

❖ Incentive Systems

Jones believed that incentive systems must meet certain criteria. Incentives:

- must be attractive enough to genuinely make the child work harder ; for example, art/watching a video;
- should abide by "grandma's rule" - first eat your dinner then you can have your dessert. Students are expected to complete the required work before going onto something they wish to do;
- should be of educational value;
- should be easily implemented;
- must be used effectively. Most teachers concentrate on rewards like early marks or stars which reward only the few top achievers, and which are not necessarily educationally sound;
- should apply to the whole class; for examples, free time for a preferred activity.

❖ Providing Efficient Help

Jones claimed that teachers spend twice as long as they estimate with each child. Teachers who were efficient in helping students had less disruption in their classrooms. There are three key aspects to efficient help:
- organising classroom seating efficiently;
- using graphic reminders that explain procedures, proper formats, etc or have worked example on the board;
- keeping individual help to a minimum time (be positive; be brief; be gone). Jones suggests about ten seconds. Go back to the student as much as needed but don't stay longer than about ten seconds each time and give the student something to go on with.

Jacob Kounin

Kounin's (1970) model has important implications for the amount of academic engaged time that exists in classrooms. His strategies are aimed at maintaining high levels of student engagement which should lead to fewer behaviour problems. In this way, Kounin's model may be seen to be more preventative than corrective. His strategies relate closely to teaching practices recommended by research into teacher effectiveness. The importance of relevant and appropriate curriculum to student management is also highlighted.

Key Concepts from the Kounin Model

❖ The "ripple effect"

Kounin coined this term to describe the manner in which teacher corrections of one student influence the behaviour of other students. The ripple effect is most powerful in primary school, less so in secondary settings.

❖ "Withitness"

This term describes the effective teacher's ability to know what is going on in all parts of the classroom. Kounin believed that students are particularly affected by a teacher who:
- is able to locate the source of a disturbance rather than a response to a disturbance;
- responds to serious incidents over minor ones;
- is able to overlap, that is, attend to two issues at once.

- ❖ *Movement management.* Teachers need to develop an understanding of:
  - *lesson pacing*, so students are neither bored nor overwhelmed;
  - *momentum*, thus avoiding "overdwelling" on discipline or unnecessary details;
  - *transitions*, to increase academic engaged time.
    NB Kounin stated that the ability to manage smooth transitions and maintain an appropriate momentum was more important to classroom management than any other behaviour management technique - a powerful assertion!

- ❖ *Group management*

Groups need to be organised to facilitate:
  - regular participation by each member, rather than everyone waiting for one member to perform;
  - accountability by all students within the group;
  - maximum attention by each member of a group. This largely depends on strategies the teacher uses, such as not identifying who will be called on to answer a question before the question is asked, not focussing on one student in responding to individual questions, and not being too predictable generally.
    NB The attention element is seen to be the most important of the three group management aspects in maintaining work involvement and preventing misbehaviour.

- ❖ *Avoiding satiation*

Avoiding "too much" of anything is achieved by:
  - visible signs of progress. Strategies such as plotting their own progress on graphs were seen to be particularly effective in demonstrating this;
  - challenge. Presenting just the right amount of challenge in an enthusiastic and positive manner prevents boredom;
  - variety. Variety in presentation style, student participation and involvement, and resources provides the appropriate stimulation to avoid student boredom.

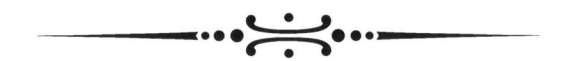

The Behaviourist Model

One of the most influential models of behaviour management, particularly of severe behaviour disorders, has emerged from the behaviourist school of thought. Behaviourist approaches arose from the work of Skinner.

Key Concepts from the Behaviourist Model

- Inappropriate behaviours are learned. What we learn depends on what behaviours are reinforced or rewarded in our everyday experiences;
- Behaviours are seen as being the result of *antecedent* events, which trigger the behaviour, and/or *consequent* events that follow the behaviour;
- In order to change disruptive behaviour, you need to ensure that undesirable behaviours are no longer rewarded and are replaced by more desirable behaviours. The application of behaviourist principles involves identifying events and objects in the environment that can be manipulated in order to change behaviour. To do this, you analyse the problem behaviours to determine what environmental factors are reinforcing them. You then change either the antecedents (those things occurring before the behaviour) or the consequences of the behaviour;
- To undertake behaviourist techniques the teacher needs three basic skills:
  - the ability to identify behaviours. The target behaviour must be described accurately and be measurable. "Aggressive behaviour" is too general. You would need to specify an action like "Hitting";
  - the ability to collect behavioural data. Four methods can be used to do this:
    i. event recording (measuring the frequency of specific behaviours);
    ii. interval recording (recording frequency of a behaviour during a particular time period);
    iii. time sampling (recording behaviour that occurs within a time sample, eg. five minutes within an interval recording time of 30 minutes);
    iv. duration recording (used when duration of behaviour is more of a concern than frequency).
  - the ability to apply reinforcers effectively. Once data has been collected the teacher must use reinforcements appropriately. The

success of behaviour intervention programs depends on the effectiveness of the use of reinforcers. Reinforcers are anything that increases the likelihood of that behaviour occurring again.

❖ Effective use of behavioural techniques demands an understanding of many key concepts. The most important for classroom teachers is an understanding of how to use reinforcers to control the consequences of behaviour. Walker and Shea (1991) outlined a number of basic guidelines for using reinforcements:
  - The reinforcer is given only when the targeted behaviour is manifested;
  - Reinforcers must be given immediately the targeted behaviour is shown;
  - During the initial stages of intervention the targeted behaviour must be reinforced every time it is exhibited;
  - Once the behaviour has been established at a satisfactory level it should be reinforced intermittently.

The principles of reinforcement are used by many teachers when they use point systems in their classrooms to reward appropriate behaviour. We will be referring to these in more detail in Chapter Six, when we discuss the use of reward systems in the classroom.

The Cognitive Behavioural Model

Dissatisfaction with a strictly behavioural approach because of the lack of thought and involvement implied; the assumption that learning is externally driven and directed; and the fact that it does not take into account the student's beliefs about why he succeeded or failed, led to development of the cognitive behavioural approach. Strategies within this model are based on a combination of cognitive and behavioural techniques which attempt to modify behaviour by changing the way students think (Whitman et al, 1991).

Key Concepts from the Cognitive-Behaviourist Model

❖ This model is aimed at increasing self-reliance and independent decision-making on the part of the students;

- ❖ Cognitive behavioural approaches are based on how language affects cognition, and on teaching students to "talk sense to themselves" (Wragg 1989). These approaches are often referred to as Cognitive Behavioural Therapy or CBT;
- ❖ CBT is based on:
  - the student becoming aware of the antecedents and consequences of his behaviour;
  - identifying a goal of more appropriate behaviour;
  - exploring alternative ways of achieving that goal;
  - developing a plan to modify that behaviour;
  - implementing the plan;
  - monitoring its success.

  Many different skills are required to be successful in this process. Students need to learn the skills of monitoring their behaviour toward a certain goal, checking outcomes and redirecting unsuccessful efforts;

- ❖ Students are taught how to monitor their own behaviour, and how to guide themselves towards the desired behaviours through the use of verbal self-instructional processes. Teachers support this process by modelling the appropriate processes or behaviours and guiding the students through each stage;

- ❖ These strategies work well with students with behaviour problems. Initially they may need to be combined with behaviour contracts, rewards and reinforcement schedules for successful completion of new behaviours. The goal is to fade external reinforcers gradually and give students the opportunity to self-evaluate their progress;

- ❖ There is also an emphasis in behavioural programs on the student changing negative or maladaptive self-talk into positive self-talk. As thinking guides behaviour, so negative thoughts will direct behaviour into destructive paths. Replacing that thinking with positive, helpful thoughts through a process of verbal self-instruction training results in more appropriate behaviour.

Psychological or Needs-based Communication Models

Alfred Adler's *Individual Psychology*

Early development of needs-based models emerged from the work of Alfred Adler (1870-1937) whose concept of *Individual Psychology* has been very influential in many models of behaviour management. Adler's contention was that everyone has a basic need to "belong" and that all behaviour can be interpreted as trying to meet this need. These attempts, however, are not always appropriate (Adler, 1957; Hall & Lindzey, 1970).

Key Concepts from Adler's Model

- Behaviour must be understood in a social context;
- Behaviour is goal directed - aimed at the future not a result of the past;
- Behaviour is chosen, not made in response to stimuli;
- Insight produces change - being aware of the reasons for our behaviour allows us to change.

Dreikurs and the *Goals of Classroom Misbehaviour*

Rudolph Dreikurs developed the ideas of Adler. Misbehaviour was seen to be caused by students' faulty beliefs about what "belonging" means and how they can achieve it. Misbehaviour is not aimless but directed at achieving certain goals (Dreikurs, 1968; Dreikurs & Cassell, 1972; Dreikurs, Grunwald & Pepper, 1982).

Key concepts from Dreikurs' Model

- Student behaviour, according to Dreikurs, was aimed at one of four outcomes:
  - **Attention seeking**, through behaviours like showing off or clowning around. Being excessively shy, untidy or excessively pleasant were also seen to be attention-seeking behaviours;
  - **Power** was sought through arguing, being unco-operative, defiant, stubborn, rebellious, contradicting the teacher, or even being extremely forgetful or slow;
  - **Revenge** was sought through stealing, being cruel, destructive and violent. Being sullen, moody or refusing to participate could also be signs of a vengeful student;

- **Escape** was sought by being lazy, helpless, or engaging in juvenile or solitary behaviour.

❖ **Appropriate Responses to Behaviour**

The same behaviour by different students could mean different things. Often the easiest way to determine the goal of the behaviour is to assess the way the behaviour makes you feel. You should redirect students to more appropriate ways of meeting their needs by not responding in the way the student wanted. Therefore you should:

- Ignore attention-seeking behaviour. Never give attention on demand, even for useful behaviour. Help students become self-motivated. Give attention in ways they don't expect;
- Refuse to engage in power struggles. Withdraw from the conflict. Let the consequences of students' behaviour occur. Win their cooperation by enlisting their help;
- Refuse to feel hurt or upset by greatly discouraged students wanting revenge, but rather convince students that they can belong by being liked and accepted. Avoid feeling hurt. Don't get hooked into seeking your own revenge. Instead work to build a trusting relationship;
- Avoid feeling discouraged by "helpless students" or giving up on them. Don't criticise or pity. Encourage any positive effort.

Dinkmeyer, McKay and Dinkmeyer's *S.T.E.T. Program*

Dreikurs' ideas were formulated into a behaviour management program called Systematic Training for Effective Teaching (the STET program) by Dinkmeyer, Dinkmeyer and McKay (1980). The S.T.E.T. program promoted a "democratic classroom" where choices are clear, discipline is logical and self-discipline is encouraged. There is a strong emphasis on communication skills. Dinkmeyer and his collegues drew on the work of Thomas Gordon and his development of the Parent Effectiveness Training (PET) (1970) and Teacher Effectiveness Training (TET) (1974, 1991) programs. These programs stressed the importance of communication skills.

Key concepts from the S.T.E.T. program

The STET program has several key features:

- **Praise versus Encouragement**

Dinkmeyer, McKay and Dinkmeyer suggest that praise can be discouraging and when we praise we send the subtle message that "You're worthwhile only when you do things well". They suggest praise is not as good as encouragement. We should avoid praising but rather help students evaluate themselves through encouragement. Praise, the authors believe, connects students' work with their personal worth, inviting fear or failure. Praise, however warm, places a value judgment on the student as a person.

Encouragement, on the other hand, focuses on the strengths of the work, helping students see and feel confident about their own abilities. It instils faith. Encouragement shows acceptance and respect.

While Dinkmeyer and colleagues raise some interesting points about how we should respond to students' work, it should be noted that not all writers in the field of behaviour management believe that praising work is a bad thing. We believe that praising student work is an important part of a multi-modal approach to behaviour management.

- **Reflective listening**

Reflective listening is encouraged in the S.T.E.T. program. You do this by paraphrasing what the student said in order to communicate the message that you are listening and understanding. You should practise reflective listening and recognise both feelings and cognitive content. Reflective listening communicates understanding of students' feelings about the problems they face. "You feel very sad because your friend says he doesn't like you anymore" would be a statement typical of reflective listening.

- **Use of "I" messages**

I-messages inform students about how their behaviour affects you. For example, (to the class) "When you are not interested in my lesson, I feel very discouraged because I've worked hard to prepare it." You-messages, on the other hand, accuse, blame, and criticize: "You'll fail if you don't hand this in." They reinforce goals of misbehaviour and may invite hostile, defensive behaviour.

I-messages report the speaker's concerns and feelings, quietly and respectfully: "When you interrupt, I get worried because we're running out of time and we need to finish." I-messages trust students to respond appropriately. I-messages are often unexpected and so usually don't reinforce goals of misbehaviour.

❖ Problem-solving conferences

Communication with difficult or hard-to-handle students should involve problem-solving conferencing in which alternatives are explored and goals of misbehaviour are disclosed. Alternatives should be explored through brainstorming. They are evaluated, a choice is made and then commitment to the solution is established. You need to help students decide how to solve a problem they own, or negotiate agreements with students for teacher-owned problems. "What are some ways you could solve your problem?" Or, "How could we settle our disagreement?"

❖ Use of natural and logical consequences

If problems occur, Dinkmeyer et al suggest the use of natural and logical consequences instead of rewards and punishment. Natural consequences allow students, within limits, to decide how they will behave and permits them to experience the results of their decisions. Natural consequences are those that follow of their own accord; for example, students who fight may get hurt. Our duty of care as teachers may prevent us from using strictly natural consequences. A young child who runs onto the road will probably get hurt – we cannot allow that natural consequence to occur.

When natural consequences are not appropriate, Dinkmeyer et al recommend the use of logical consequences rather than punishment. Punishment is not recommended because it:
- expresses the power of personal authority;
- may be quite unrelated to the nature of the misbehaviour;
- implies a moral judgement;
- is concerned about past behaviour;
- may increase conflict;
- removes responsibility from the student;
- impedes development of self-discipline.

Logical consequence, on the other hand:
- express the reality of the social order;
- acknowledge mutual rights;

- are directly related to the misbehaviour;
- are concerned with present and future behaviour.

❖ Use of Class meetings

Democratic forums should be used to promote the sharing of ideas, feelings and opinions of others and to plan policies, guidelines etc, to solve problems and to encourage positive problem solving. Guidelines for meetings include:
- adhere to time limits;
- become an equal group member with students;
- strive for consensus. Put agreements into action;
- don't allow anyone to monopolize meetings;
- don't permit meetings to become gripe sessions;
- block personal attacks;
- evaluate meetings periodically.

Maurice Balson

Maurice Balson, an Australian, also developed the notions of Dreikurs into an approach to behaviour management (1992). Because people's basic need is to belong, Balson believed teachers need to concentrate on modifying motivation rather than behaviour. Because behaviour is purposeful, knowledge of the goal of the behaviour is important if we want to influence that behaviour

Key Concepts from Balson

- ❖ Problems occur in classrooms because teachers do not have a psychological understanding of student behaviour. Behaviour must be viewed as students' efforts to belong to the classroom and behaviour always makes sense to the student;
- ❖ Children attempt to find a place for themselves by whatever behaviours are available. They are not concerned whether these are socially useful or socially useless. Teachers need to *change the belief* that generates the emotion necessary for the behaviour, rather than focus on what they believe to be inappropriate behaviour;
- ❖ Schools create many behaviour problems through the harmful practices of grading and withdrawal and through a competition-driven approach to learning. Changes in society demand a change in the way we respond to and interact with students. Democratic principles

like social equality, mutual respect, shared responsibility, co-operation and self-discipline must be incorporated within schooling systems;
* The use of co-operative learning techniques rather than competitive methods will reduce behaviour problems;
* Encouragement rather than praise will reduce behaviour problems;
* Self discipline will develop through the use of natural and logical consequences over punishment.

Balson was one of the first people to specifically highlight the importance of effective teaching within a classroom management model. He recommended a mastery learning approach be used: a highly systematic and individualised instructional approach which is usually used for students in special education programs. Students do not progress until they have achieved mastery to a very high level in all basic material. He believed this approach would ensure that all students would learn to a high standard and many discipline problems would be averted.

Balson was also concerned with the stress that classroom management problems caused teachers and included specific stress reduction strategies in the last edition of his book.

William Glasser's *Choice Theory*

Glasser was a psychiatrist who applied many of his ideas to school contexts. He believes motivation comes from within, and arises in response to our five basic needs:
- survival;
- love and belonging;
- power (self determination);
- fun and excitement;
- freedom and independence.

Glasser's major contribution to understanding behaviour disorders has been the application of "Control Theory" to student management (1969). Control theory was renamed "Choice Theory" in the 1990s (1998). Glasser originally outlined a ten-step approach to discipline (1977), as seen in Box 5.1, but revised a number of his ideas in later writings (1993, 1998).

Box 5.1 Glasser's Original 10 Step Behaviour Management Plan

1. What am I doing? (look at what you as the teacher are doing)
2. Is it working? (change what you are doing)
3. Catch the child being good.
4. Ask the child "What are you doing?"
5. Ask the child, "Is what you're doing helping you? Is it against the rules?"
6. We've got to work it out (set time aside to talk to the student – make a plan).
7. If the student is not willing to make a plan, isolate him within the classroom (the child becomes a passive listener and therefore not a fully participating class member).
8. School time out area (Someone on the staff should ask the child if he is ready to work it out).
9. Sent home (this changed in Glasser's later writing when he was reluctant to involve home in school problems, but believed teacher and student should work it out together).
10. Offer outside professional help (refer on if child needs professional counselling).

Key Concepts from Glasser's model

- ❖ Glasser rejects the belief that behaviour is directed by external influence. He believes people behave only to meet their needs;
- ❖ Past events can never be used to excuse irresponsible behaviour. Full responsibility must be taken for present behaviour, even though past events may have left a student with a limited repertoire of ways to satisfy his needs;
- ❖ Students must become aware of their behaviour and whether or not that behaviour is likely to meet their needs. Students are asked to commit themselves to new ways of behaving to meet their needs more appropriately;
- ❖ Glasser rejects the notion of mental illness. Our personalities are simply our way of behaving to meet our needs and are amenable to change;
- ❖ We need to focus on quality education. We need to reduce content and give more students a better grasp of basics;
- ❖ Schools are not part of the "quality world" of most students, who find school boring and unsatisfying. Schools do not meet students' needs, nor do most students believe that their teachers care about

them. Discipline problems occur with students who have great difficulty having their needs met in school. Students need to receive a strong 'We care' message from their teachers;
- A successful teacher is one who can convince all of his students to do quality work in school. Schools are not encouraging divergent thinking, creativity or constructive thought about social issues. The curriculum is essentially irrelevant for most students;
- Grades should only be used to show students what they know. Students should be encouraged to grade their own work, as Choice Theory contends that students would be reluctant to assess one of their own assignments as being of low quality - they would rather work harder and give themselves a deservedly higher grade;
- Homework is a main reason for students taking school out of their quality world. Schools should concentrate on quality schoolwork done with their support and direction;
- The function of schools is to teach students this important rule:

   The success or failure of our lives is greatly dependent on our willingness to judge the quality of what we do and then to improve it if we find it wanting.

- Schools need to move from *boss management* to *lead management*.

  Boss managers:
  - set tasks and standards without consultation;
  - tell rather than show;
  - designate, inspect, grade;
  - use coercion.

  Lead managers:
  - engage the workers in discussion of work;
  - show or model the job;
  - ask workers to evaluate their own work;
  - facilitate rather than coerce.

An Eclectic Model

Bill Rogers' *Decisive Discipline*

Bill Rogers (1989; 1993; 1994; 1995; 1998) discriminates between decisive and indecisive teachers. Indecisive teachers "have unclear rules and expectations and thus are regularly tested. They model uncertainty in their posture and voice and have great difficulty asserting their appropriate authority.... These teachers adopt an 'us versus them', win-lose attitude. The net result is that the student's rights are trampled and the students know it" (Tauber, 1995).

Decisive teachers "recognize that they cannot make students do anything. Instead, their verbal language and body language convey an expectation that their reasonable requests will be followed. Their language is brief (thus avoiding over-servicing a student's bids for attention or power), clear and directed, rule focused, calm and businesslike, and assertive when the situation demands it" (Tauber, 1995).

Bill Rogers incorporates elements from several different approaches. There are aspects of a needs model in his emphasis on disciplining respectfully and restoring good relationships with students. There is a strong management focus in his use of rules, routines and a hierarchy of corrective strategies. There are behaviourist elements in his use of consequences.

Key Concepts from Bill Rogers' model

- Classroom management should exist within a framework of reciprocal rights and responsibilities of teacher and students;
- Jointly develop rules with students;
- Develop a clear classroom management plan (hierarchical) and work from least to most intrusive;
- Intentionally minimize embarrassment and discipline respectfully;
- Use positive language as much as possible, eg., "Working, thanks", rather then "Stop talking";
- Provide appropriate choices e.g. either you do "X" or "consequence";
- Plan classroom management as carefully as the curriculum;
- Avoid responding to secondary behaviour (the arguing, pouting or sulking that follows a redirection to task);
- Schools have a responsibility to develop system-wide approaches for the very difficult students.

Rogers provides a comprehensive list of management strategies that may be employed throughout the phases of a lesson. These range from low level strategies such as tactical ignoring, proximity control and casual refocusing; to medium level strategies such as clear directions and rule restatements; to higher level strategies such as offering simple choices and high key commands. He suggests a cue system may be needed for dangerous students who refuse to leave the classroom.

Rogers also provides guidelines for developing contracts with difficult students; the establishment of class meetings, welfare support groups, behaviour rehearsals, peer support programs and conflict resolution meetings. In the most extreme cases teachers need a crisis plan for out-of-control children.

Each of the models or approaches presented in this chapter has contributed to the body of knowledge about how best to manage disruptive behaviour. We have learned something from each of them, as well as from many years' experience as either a classroom teacher, a specialist teacher of students with behaviour problems or a guidance counsellor.

We will now continue with our own response to disruptive behaviour within classrooms. It forms part of our overall structured approach to managing classroom behaviour which must include:
- an understanding of the individual needs of students;
- an awareness of strategies to create a positive learning environment;
- the development of effective rules and routines;
- a knowledge of sound teaching procedures;
- a working knowledge of existing models of behaviour management, particularly those that have proved to be effective;
- specific strategies to manage off-task and disruptive behaviour in the classroom;
- a recognition that, on some occasions, teachers need to move outside the classroom to work with individual students with greater behavioural needs;
- an awareness of how managing difficult behaviours can affect teachers' thoughts and beliefs about their own effectiveness;

❖ proactive strategies to combat the stress that teaching involves.

We have already addressed the first five points, stressing the importance of the planning and preparation stage, implementing effective practice and using the collective wisdom of those who have gone before us. Chapters Six, Seven and Eight will explore the final four points.

PART THREE

Facing Squalls and Heavy Swells

Chapter Six

RESPONDING TO DIFFICULT BEHAVIOURS: CLASSROOM STRATEGIES

Introduction

We have already discussed the fact that effective classroom managers develop rules collaboratively with their students, and implement strong routines from the beginning of the year. These are strategies that should establish a positive learning environment and prevent many time-wasting and disruptive behaviours from occurring.

The fact is, however, that on some occasions, no matter how well prepared you are, nor how efficient the functioning of your classroom, on some occasions students will need redirection to task and correction of behaviour. *You need to have a plan* for how you will manage situations of this kind. It is as important to plan for classroom management as it is to plan for curriculum content.

Before discussing some general principles of behaviour change and specific strategies to facilitate behaviour change, we need to mention a critical point about behaviour that you need to consider when developing your responses to management difficulties in the classroom.

> **The only behaviour you can really control is your own!**

If you are unhappy with what is going on in the classroom, firstly look at what *you* are doing. Your behaviour is directly under your control and therefore the easiest to change. If classroom management problems have been long-term, you clearly need to change something because current strategies are not being successful. There is little point in approaching the problem with an attitude of "Why should I have to change what I'm doing?

I'm meant to be the one in charge. These kids just have to shape up, respect me and get on with their work."

Systems Theory (von Bertalanffy, 1968; Bronfenbrenner, 1979) tells us that a change in one element of any environment, will inevitably lead to changes in other elements of that environment. The various elements of any classroom are constantly interacting and affecting each other. It just may be that a relatively small change in your behaviour can result in quite significant changes in classroom functioning. Look to yourself first!

Principles of Behaviour Correction

Begin with the lowest level strategies

The mistake that many inexperienced teachers make is to begin with the high level strategy of raising the voice as soon as a student moves off task. There are much less intrusive strategies that are available and which we will discuss later in this chapter.

Discipline respectfully

When students misbehave or stop working, they do not automatically lose their right to your respect. It is important (and more effective) to avoid embarrassing the student concerned. Most children of all ages are sensitive to the rebukes of a "power" figure such as a teacher. You should never use your power to humiliate a student, nor to deliberately embarrass or cause a student to lose face. This becomes even more critical when dealing with adolescents, for whom a loss of face is a serious issue. Strategies such as a sarcastic retort, or a heavy-handed loudly-voiced command, are far more likely to escalate the situation into a power struggle if a student feels he is likely to lose face with his peers.

Use positive before punitive strategies

Low level strategies that simply redirect the student and emphasise what the student should be doing should always be used before a consequence is applied. The tone of a classroom can be greatly affected by the percentages of positive and negative statements that occur. Research shows that teachers habitually use more negative than positive statements throughout a school day (Elton Report, 1989). Try to increase the number of positive statements and strategies that you use to reverse this trend.

Provide choices whenever possible

As we mentioned previously, it is almost impossible to make someone over about the age of two do something that he is determined not to do. By allowing students choice, they can save face and you can avoid a power struggle. It is not really a choice if you are standing over him, counting to three while you wait for compliance. You need to allow a reasonable "take-up time", while you get back to work with the rest of the class.

Nip it in the bud

If you monitor effectively, you will rapidly become aware when students are not doing what they should be. It is important to intervene quickly, before a higher level response may be required. You will also learn what situations or "triggers" are likely to lead to disruption. Don't wait until a difficult situation has emerged before making a pre-emptive strike!

Don't over-react

A very common cause of trouble in secondary classrooms is unintentional swearing. If a student accidentally knocks something off his desk as he is organising materials, he may well mutter "sh&%". Some swear words have become nothing more than a convenient adjective that is placed before many nouns, and is not intended as a term of abuse nor is it a signal of someone losing control. By not over-reacting to the use of swearing in these circumstances, it is easier to restore a working atmosphere. While you should make it clear that such language is inappropriate in the classroom, it is not worth a massive over-reaction that wastes further teaching time and has the potential to escalate into a major issue. (Please note that we are not advocating a tolerant response to abusive swearing directed at other students or to you. These are far more serious issues and require a higher level response.)

Stay calm

Getting angry in a classroom *never* works long-term! This is a strong statement and one that we make quite deliberately. Some authors suggest that occasionally "losing your cool" is a useful strategy. *Acting* like you're angry may work occasionally. But you should never place yourself in a position where you may lose control, and getting angry is one such situation. This is not to say that you should never speak firmly and assertively, and some behaviours are so unacceptable that you need to express just that in very strong terms. You need to remain in control of your emotions even if for no other reason than to model appropriate ways to address a problem.

Avoid responding to secondary behaviour

Some students are masterful in sidetracking teachers. When you are directing students back to task, concentrate on that. Often a student will begin explaining, blaming someone else, or bringing up an unrelated matter. It is so easy to allow yourself to be sidetracked in this way. If your direction has been to 'Get back to your summary, now, Garry', and Garry starts saying something like 'But I was only…" or "But Stephanie took….' or some such thing, you need to concentrate on getting Garry back to his summary. Blocking is sometimes an effective strategy in these cases. Keep repeating the first direction each time the student tries to distract you.

There are a couple of important provisos here. Firstly, getting back to work should be reasonable and possible for Garry; he should be able to do the work (that is, the material should be relevant and interesting, matched to his ability level), and he should have all necessary equipment (so these organisational matters should have been sorted out previously). You can see that a large part of this is up to you as the teacher.

The other important proviso is that the blocking is done in a pleasant manner, even with a smile on the face, that communicates to the student the fact that you're onto him, and he's not getting away with it. It is very easy for this strategy to become quite aggressive if said loudly or in an irritated tone.

Some students may indulge in rolling the eyes heavenward (an adolescent girl speciality!), pulling a face, or giving an enormous sigh as they reluctantly get on with it. These, too, are secondary behaviours. It is very tempting to become irritated by these behaviours, comment on them, or begin some harangue about lack of respect, etc, etc. A simple "Thank you" with a smile (but don't make it smug!) is more effective and less likely to waste further class time.

Occasionally the secondary behaviour is more serious. If, for example, a student has been continually out of his chair, and you have directed him back to his desk, he may well move back slowly, knocking something, perhaps a ruler, off another student's desk on his way in order to save face and show who's really boss! He has in fact done what you asked, that is, moved back to his desk. But he is attempting to further distract you and this may even be a major "call to battle". It is very easy for a situation like this to escalate into a power struggle if you over-react to his secondary behaviour. In these situations it is important to defuse the situation. Pick up the item that was knocked off the desk and say "Thanks for going back, Garry...we'll talk about the ruler later." You are thereby acknowledging that he has done what you asked (after a fashion) but you are not going to waste further class time on it. You are also letting Garry and, importantly, the rest of the class, know that he is not going to get away with it.

If the student does something even more serious, such as "accidentally" kicking a student on the way, you would need to address the matter immediately. This would warrant exiting the student from the room.

Always follow-up

If you say you will be seeing a student out of class, it is critical that you do just that. The school grapevine will quickly identify you as a "pushover" if you fail to do this, and classroom problems will be multiplied in the playground as students in other classes take advantage of this. It is worth the lack of coffee break/lunch/preparation time in the short term for the long-term respect this practice will bring you.

Choosing to spend your time in this way also sends a powerful message to the students. You are, in fact, giving them the message that they are worth more to you than that cup of coffee; that you see it as a worthwhile use of your time to solve the problem you are both having. You may be the first teacher who has given this message!

Be on their side

When you have a difficult student in your class, it is very important that the student gets the clear impression that you are on his side, that you care about him as a person and his progress at school. It is not always easy to like every student, but it makes an enormous difference to a student if he truly believes that you like him and want him to do well. We have all seen teachers who, by their behaviour, make it clear that they do not like a particular student. In that case, there is little incentive for the student to take note of what the teacher says, whether it concern learning or behaviour.

Always reward appropriate behaviour

Some teachers who become concerned about the level of off-task and disruptive behaviour in their classrooms take little time to ensure that they are acknowledging and positively reinforcing appropriate behaviours when they occur. You could use some of the strategies which are suggested in the following section to reward the students when they are doing the correct thing. This is especially important for those students who are more inclined to be disruptive.

Reward Systems

Introduction

Although your aim is to develop in your students a self-motivating, intrinsic desire to learn and interact with others positively, it is often necessary to have in place some sort of reward or incentive system to use with students who have not yet learned to do these things. Indeed, many teachers have reward systems operating in their classrooms throughout the year before any particularly difficult behaviours occur. Individual or group point systems are typical examples of these. Parents often use similar systems to encourage their children to do their piano practice, to eat their vegetables or even to do homework.

Students who find it difficult to conform to acceptable standards of group behaviour are usually those who benefit most from such systems. The more difficult the behaviours, the more likely it will be that you will need some reward system operating in your classroom. Students whose behaviour is guided by external factors, who are not yet guided by intrinsic motivation, often need an incentive system, or a carefully planned system of rewards, to help shape their behaviour towards more acceptable forms. We will now provide some information about how incentive systems work, and how you can implement them most effectively.

Developing Incentive Systems

Incentive systems are based on the behaviourist principle of *reinforcement*. As we mentioned in Chapter Five, a reinforcer is anything that occurs immediately after a behaviour that increases the likelihood of that behaviour occurring again. Being paid for work increases the likelihood that an employee will continue to work. Receiving acknowledgement for staying on task or behaving appropriately is also rewarding for most students. This increases the chance that they will continue to stay on task.

Some people believe that using reinforcement is akin to bribery and should never be used. Yet receiving a reward for doing something well is how most of the world operates. Adults receive a wage for working and this is not considered to be bribing adults to turn up for work. The simple fact is that people respond positively to rewards, and continue to do those things that they find are rewarded.

Understanding Reinforcers

Reinforcers are effective tools in a classroom if they are understood and used appropriately. To be most effective in increasing appropriate behaviour, they must be used in the following way.

> They must follow **immediately** after the desired behaviour. This is especially important for students who are having trouble conforming to school rules, and who need a strong motivator.
> They must be **frequent**, especially in the early stages when a strong reinforcement schedule is necessary. Frequent reinforcement is also necessary when you are trying to teach a new behaviour or skill.
> They must be **highly desired** or strong reinforcers. You need to ensure that the "reward" is truly reinforcing for the student(s) concerned. You can also increase the desirability of a reinforcer by building it up, and referring to it with enthusiasm and energy.

Implementing Incentive Schemes

Find out what the students like

The best way to determine what students find reinforcing is to ask them! Teachers aren't always the best judge of what students find rewarding. Remember, if a reward you have prepared doesn't result in the desired behaviour increasing, it is not reinforcing.

You could ask your students to complete a reinforcement survey which lists a number of different reinforcers that could be used in the classroom, and space for students to come with their own ideas. Teachers can read out a list to students who cannot read, or prepare the reinforcement survey using pictures rather than a long list of words.

Use the reinforcer in association with a social reinforcer

As you give the reward, smile and give lots of positive social approval, so that these less tangible social reinforcers are also associated with the desired behaviour. Your aim should be to reduce the need for tangible rewards as soon as possible. Some children may not receive many positive comments or other forms of social reinforcement at home, so these strategies can be quite effective at school. Consciously making positive comments also helps to promote a more positive atmosphere in their classrooms.

Reward often in the early stages

When setting up your reward program, you need to reward appropriate behaviour often in the early stages. This is also the case if trying to teach new behaviours.

Describe the desired behaviour

The students need to know exactly why they are being rewarded. Describe the behaviour that earned the reward. If several students in the class have problem behaviours, you may have greater success targeting just one behaviour at a time. You may decide to concentrate on students staying in their seats and specifically reward that behaviour in a "behaviour blitz".

Monitor the use of the reinforcer

You may need to change the reinforcer regularly to maintain the behaviour. Because something works well once, it does not mean it won't need changing. Once something stops being effective, it is no longer a reinforcer.

Fade the tangible reinforcer gradually

While social praise may continue indefinitely, you may be able to reduce the level of artificial or tangible reinforcers. You will probably have to do this very gradually for difficult behaviours. The effort put into maintaining effective reinforcement programs is worth it when one considers the amount of time disruptive behaviour causes.

Use natural reinforcers where possible

Daily life in schools contains many natural reinforcers that can be used by teachers. Being first in a line, being a class monitor, being the class messenger, sitting at the teacher's desk, sitting with a friend, being a buddy to a younger grade member, listening to music in the classroom, can all act as rewards when students behave appropriately. They also have the advantage of costing nothing!

Not all activities will be rewarding to all students. Teachers who know their students well are more likely to devise and offer rewards that will work.

Use tangible reinforcers when necessary

Tangible reinforcers are concrete rewards such as food, stickers, toys, stationery items, etc. The ever-increasing number of shops which sell liquidated stock at greatly reduced prices are very useful sources of such rewards. Teachers can easily accumulate a supply of tangible (and tax-deductible) rewards such as magnets, small torches, coloured markers, balls of varying types, all kinds of stationery sets, badges, stickers, pencil cases, erasers, bags of marbles, small books, magnifying glasses, animal ornaments, wind chimes, glitter pens, magic markers, riddle and joke books, candles, nail polish, and hair accessories. Prizes for older students can include blank video and cassette tapes, but in our experience even adolescents are still quite susceptible to such things as snack bars.

We will now talk about some specific strategies you can use to direct students back to task and avoid minor problems becoming major ones. These strategies flesh out the principles mentioned above, with an emphasis on using lower level strategies first, maintaining respect for your students at all times, and operating on the basis of getting students back to work as quickly as possible.

Suggestions for Class and Individual Reward Systems

Students who need strong reinforcement schedules respond well to systems that build gradually to a bigger reward. Prizes can be directed at individuals or at groups. Individuals can win privileges or prizes for the whole class. This ensures that the peers will be helpful and encouraging towards the targeted student.

Marble Jar

Reward students for responding quickly to a call to attention, for on-task behaviour, for staying in seats, or whatever behaviour you are targeting by placing a marble inside a clear jar when the behaviour occurs. When a predetermined number has been collected, the class receives a prize like a special morning tea, an afternoon of free choice activity, or watching a video.

Dot-to-dot Rewards

The actual prize, (a canteen voucher, a skateboarding magazine, a snack bar) may be represented in a dot-to-dot sketch which is won when all dots have been joined. The student is rewarded for appropriate behaviour by being allowed to join two of the dots. The student can track his progress towards the final goal.

Ladders to Heaven

A sketch of a ladder could be used to reinforce a student several times on the way to a major prize which sits at the top of the ladder. As the student reaches certain rungs on the ladder, a smaller reward is received.

Prize Surprise

Write the name of a prize on a piece of paper and place it inside an envelope. Place an **X** on the front of the envelope and cover it with a peel off sticker or piece of masking tape. Then place several more peel off stickers all over the envelope. Students earn the right to peel off one sticker. If no **X** is revealed, they must wait for another chance to peel off a sticker. When the **X** is revealed they are allowed the 'Prize Surprise'.

Spinning wheels

Several different rewards could be placed in different sections of a spinner. Students earn a spin by behaving in a certain way for a certain period of time. All of the activities listed should be genuinely reinforcing for the student(s) concerned. If some are more valuable than others, the sections in the circle can be varying widths, so the chance of winning the most highly valued prize is lessened.

Mystery bags

A highly coloured bag could contain several wrapped prizes for a lucky dip when students have earned a certain number of tokens.

Raffle tickets

You distribute one half of a raffle ticket every time you want to reinforce behaviour. At the end of the period/day/week, all raffle tickets stubs are placed in a box and tickets are drawn for prizes. The more the students need reinforcing, the more often you need to draw a ticket.

All raffle tickets can go back in the box for weekly or monthly drawings for slightly bigger prizes. A "fine" system can also be built into a draw by not calling out the name of any student who has been "disqualified" for particularly inappropriate behaviour. It is not necessary to call out the student's name – the teacher just mentions it is someone who has been disqualified from the drawer and draws another name. If there is more than one disqualified student, any one of them could have collected the prize.

Raffle tickets are widely available and inexpensive. Otherwise, more individualised tickets can be made up using a computer.

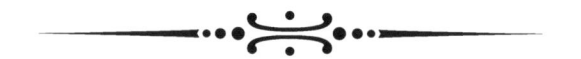

The number of different ways that you can incorporate rewards into the daily routine is limited only by your imagination. You may always need to have some sort of reward system in place. That is better than having reduced teaching time. Along with an incentive system, however, you also need to have clearly defined strategies for use when students need redirection. We will now discuss some specific strategies for managing various levels of difficult behaviour.

First Line of In-Class Defence

Thank students doing the correct thing

If you see a student not working, thank and/or reward one or two students who *are* doing the correct thing, preferably nearby. This can have the effect of bringing the off-task student back on track without any explicit direction. It also adds to the "positives" in the classroom.

Pause

A judicious pause is often enough to redirect students. This is particularly useful for students who want to continue having a private conversation rather than those students whose aim it is to seek attention. On-task students will look usually around to see the object of your gaze which adds a little peer pressure to the strategy.

Give a "teacher look"

Even without a meaningful pause, eye contact can give quite direct messages, as can raised eyebrows, a nod, or a smile. These are useful with some students, usually the more compliant and less difficult. Adolescents tend to be less predictable in their responses. The more assertive of them are quite happy to "eyeball" you back (or give you the wide-eyed and hurt look of a total innocent who has been wrongfully accused!) Nevertheless, teachers can still send important messages to many students with a look alone.

Name the student

Just the simple naming of a student is another very low key but effective strategy. Often nothing more needs to be done – the student knows you are "onto him". The importance of this strategy is highlighted by the problems faced by casual or supply teachers. Not knowing the names of students makes classroom management much more difficult. Refer to the end of Chapter Three for some specific strategies for casual teachers.

Use Proximity

Your physical presence will often be enough to redirect the student who cannot resist continuing a discussion or who is very slow in settling down to work. This is another of the multitude of reasons why teachers should continually move around the room and monitor while students are engaged in independent or group work. It is very easy then to move towards a source (or potential source) of disruption or off-task behaviour.

There is also evidence that directions given relatively close-up (1–2 metres) are more likely to be complied with. A direction given from some distance away has to be louder for a start, and so a higher key response than is required from closer quarters.

Gentle reminders

Being close also enables you to use gentle reminders or what Bill Rogers (1989) refers to as the *casual refocus*, such as

"How's it going?" *or*
"Do you understand what you have to do?" *or*
"Everything OK?"

These are all very low key ways of saying, "Why aren't you working?" or "Start working, please" and are very useful for low-level off-task behaviours. You should note, however, that for the habitual work-avoider, the easily distracted or more disruptive student, a more direct request is necessary.

Second Line of In-Class Defence

Clear directions

These are sometimes referred to as *precision statements* (Rhode et al, 1992). When using a precision statement, you express a single request exactly and positively in a calm but firm manner.

"Katie, back to your seat, please."
"Jason, turn off the bunsen burner."

It is important at this point to ensure the student begins to comply. If the student does as he is told within five to ten seconds, he is thanked, and/or rewarded if compliance is a targeted behaviour for that student.

If the student does not comply, the request is repeated once. If the student then complies, he is thanked. If the student does not comply, a pre-planned and known consequence should be applied. This would relate to the consequences discussed when class rules were developed (see Chapter Three).

Repeating the same request more than twice has not been found to be effective. "Nagging" teachers do not receive high levels of compliance. It is also more effective to give just one direction at a time, and wait until that is done, before giving another.

Refer to Rules

An important reason for having class rules on display is for referral. "Paul, remember the rule for getting my attention?" reminds the student that there is a rule, agreed upon by the class, and that he's not using it.

Another way to refer to the rule is to ask the student for the appropriate rule. "Paul, what's the rule for getting my attention?" This is easily answered if the rules are displayed prominently. If the student doesn't know, or has forgotten the rule, this is a good time to draw his attention to it.

We also like what Bill Rogers (1989) refers to as the two "magic questions": "What are you doing?" If the response is, "Nothing" (which is very common), the next question,
"What should you be doing?" either reminds the student or gives the teacher the opportunity to tell the student again.

Offer a clear choice (Yellow card)

At this point you are "upping the ante" and becoming more assertive, but you are still offering the student the opportunity to comply, rather than initiating a power struggle by insisting he follow your directions. "Stephen, either stop talking or you'll have to move". The student is then able to choose the favoured alternative without losing face – he has simply decided he will now stop talking. He has not been coerced by the teacher.

It is important that the alternative is enforceable if that is the choice the student makes. There is little point in saying, "Either you stop talking or you're never coming back to my class again." There is little chance of that happening and you will do nothing but reinforce your own powerlessness.

You can physically show a yellow card to a student as a sign that the consequences will be enforced the next time. This is a well known strategy from soccer with which most students will be familiar. It is also a reminder that rules apply in all walks of life – no-one is immune!

If, for some reason, the situation has already escalated to the point where you suspect that the student will not comply, it is better to make the alternate choice a follow-up outside the classroom. Thus, "Sarah, sit down in your seat now or we'll have to talk about this after class," tells Sarah and the class that a consequence will follow if the student continues to behave in a defiant manner. If follow-up talks are becoming a regular occurrence, some of the out-of-class strategies for more difficult behaviours which are discussed in the next chapter should be employed.

Final Line of In-Class Defence

Enforce consequences

If the previous forms of redirection have not been successful, you will need to enforce the known consequences, in order for your classroom to return to order. If students have been given a choice, and they have chosen to continue with off-task or inappropriate behaviour, the consequences must be applied. During class discussions of rules, consequences should have been discussed, so the student should be aware of what will happen. The consequences should be natural or logical if possible, that is, related to the "offence" as closely as possible.

In-class separation

Although it is difficult in some classrooms because of the room size and the number of students, removal of the student to a place which is as separate as possible, but still under your supervision, is the final line of defence within the classroom. This is not strictly time-out because there will be reinforcement still available to the student. It is also desirable that the student be given the chance to continue with the work.

Removal from the class

If the student is threatening the safety of you or other students, or is continuing to affect the learning of other students, he needs to be excluded from the group. The way that this is done must adhere to school policy. If students are asked to leave the classroom, there should be a known procedure concerning where the student goes and under whose supervision he will be.

If a student refuses to leave the classroom, the school needs to have a policy about how that student's removal from the group is managed. Most classrooms now have a red card which hangs on the doorknob or close to the door. On it is written something like:

We need an adult in Room 34 immediately.

This is sent with a reliable student to the nominated person, usually an executive member of staff or a buddy teacher.

When that person arrives, he asks the student to accompany him so that the matter can be sorted out. Amazingly, the student will often accompany another person, perhaps because that person has been removed from the emotional "heat" of the exchange. If the student still refuses to leave, one option is for you to leave the room with the other students. This can be managed in a couple of ways.

You can leave the classroom as a group and relocate to the library, hall, empty classroom or predetermined place. Another strategy is to approach students individually or in small groups and ask them to leave the room and wait for you in the predetermined place. This would then leave the executive teacher to negotiate with the student without the benefit of an audience. This changes the dynamics of the exchange quite significantly.

You should never attempt to physically remove a student of any age. Apart from the fact that this is a very difficult and undignified process, and you may well be unsuccessful, you can place yourself at great risk of legal consequences. The only time direct physical intervention may be appropriate is when the physical safety of you or your students is seriously and immediately at risk.

Monitor your physical response

When the dynamics of the classroom are becoming increasingly tense, it is very important that you are aware of what your body is doing. Whether you realise it or not, your body will probably have tensed, resulting in raised shoulders and possibly clenched fists. Your face will have reddened. Your breathing will be irregular. Consciously go through the following routine:

- relax body
- drop shoulders
- breathe out
- open hands

This routine is worth remembering and practising. Before you raise your voice or whenever you feel your blood rising, go through this routine. It will reduce the physical impact of the situation on your body. It will also give you a few seconds to reconsider your response.

The aftermath

Major disruptions to class routine have a significant effect on the student concerned, on the other students, and on you. It is your responsibility to restore the emotional order in the classroom as soon as possible. Resuming teaching is a good start. Getting back to work quickly often relieves the tension considerably. Now is not the time for any debriefing that may, in some cases, be necessary. Debriefing should be done when there is less emotional heat evident.

It is also your responsibility (remember, you're the adult!) to resume a working relationship with the student who has been removed. You need to "get over" any resentment you may feel at the student's disruption of your class. Incidents of this nature can be used as learning opportunities to model to the class continued respect for the student and how to resume good working relationships within the classroom.

Situations of this severity obviously demand follow-up strategies outside the classroom. You need to talk to the student concerned, and put in place some kind of individual behaviour program that will help the student monitor his own behaviour, learn more appropriate ways of registering his anger or resistance and hopefully learn new self-management skills. This may involve entering into an individual behaviour contract or a more closely monitored incentive system.

We will look at each of these aspects of following-up individual student behaviour outside the classroom in the next chapter.

PART FOUR

SURVIVING STORMS AT SEA

Chapter Seven

Responding to More Difficult Behaviours: Moving Outside the Classroom

Introduction

The earlier chapters have examined the importance of understanding how different each of your individual students may be, of establishing a positive emotional tone in the classroom, of using effective instructional procedures, developing routines, and using a carefully developed set of approaches to management. This chapter assumes that all of these early preparation and management stages have taken place. In this chapter we are concerned with the problem that exists when classroom management procedures have been appropriate, but some students continue to be highly disruptive.

What teachers normally do

The students we are talking about in this chapter are those that really stand out from the others. When faced with continually disruptive behaviour, most teachers use the same techniques they have used before – just more intensively. They give the student more directions, increase the volume of their commands, make the tone more critical, adopt a more intense style of monitoring, or punish more often.

Sometimes these increases in volume and tone are sufficient to move the misbehaving student back into acceptable behaviour but in many cases teachers finds themselves in a repetitive cycle. The class is instructed to do something, the student does not comply, the teacher increases volume and often proximity to the wayward student, the student starts to comply but within 30 seconds is off task again and so the cycle recommences. The cycle is then repeated many times throughout the school day. The difficult behaviours do not change; they may even have been strengthened.

At this stage it is vital to change tactics and recognise that the difficult student needs more than constant correction. You need to work with some students differently. You need to provide an individually developed educational plan that recognises how this student is different.

The *Punishment Paradox*

The research literature identifies the fact that using constant correction and punishment is not effective with students who come from homes where they are often shouted at and methods of coercion are employed to manage their behaviour. Patterson (1982), identified what he termed the *punishment paradox*. When a teacher punishes a student, or corrects him, there is often an immediate response when the student does what he has been told. This may continue for a week or two and so it appears that punishment or correction is working. However, the corrections become more frequent and the teacher spends increasing time and energy on a constantly re-occurring problem. The student may be moved from his desk to a desk that is right next to the teacher and proximity as well as continued corrections are employed. Soon the teacher is virtually the student's full-time manager.

Patterson makes the important point that punishment only works for a very short time because the student becomes *habituated* towards constant correction and constant reprimands. The corrections lose their effect. Over-correction and punishment fail in the long term. In the process, the teacher's behaviour in relation to correction or punishment increases in intensity. Finally the teacher feels defeated and gives up attempts at behaviour correction, and if possible, passes the problem on to someone else. The student/teacher relationship has usually broken down completely.

Strategies to deal with more disruptive behaviour

While you will probably need to continue with incentive and reward programs within the classroom to change really difficult or persistent behaviours, you also need to begin working with the student outside the classroom. The student needs to develop levels of self awareness, self monitoring and self-directed change. New behaviours need to be shaped. We are going to discuss several different strategies that are recommended when dealing with more difficult behaviour.

1. **Analyse the problem situation**
2. **Conduct a private talk**

3. Set up a cueing system
4. Use timers to monitor behaviour
5. Set up a monitoring program
6. Rehearse desired behaviours
7. Shape desired behaviours
8. Draw up a contract

1. Analyse the problem situation

The first step in approaching a serious problem is to spend some time actually analysing the context of problem behaviour. Use a checklist like that in Box 7.1. Does it always occur at a particular time or place? Who are the main players? Are certain students always involved?

Answering these questions often allows you to identify triggers or contexts that are particularly problematic. Try to identify the most common sequence of events. Note how you react and how you manage each stage of the scenario until it reaches the final conclusion. Try to identify any triggers that precede the undesirable behaviour. Also note how other students behave. Is the behaviour exhibited by the "target" student a reaction to something that has just happened? Who else is drawn into the behaviour sequence? How do you think the student is being reinforced by the behaviour? Do you believe the way you are responding to the behaviour is somehow reinforcing the student? Is the student receiving reinforcement from another source? Is it is a one-act play or a play spread over several frustrating and emotionally draining scenes?

Once you have done the analysis, see if any triggers or antecedent events can be changed, or if you can stop certain behaviours being reinforced. Can you interrupt the cycle of events in some way? Can you find a reinforcer that may encourage more productive replacement behaviour?

The problem analysis may clarify several points about the behaviour for you. It may also help you approach a talk with the student with a clearer understanding of what is happening. Nevertheless, keep an open mind and be prepared to accept new ideas that may emerge from your discussion.

Box 7.1 Analysis of Problem Behaviours Checklist

Setting in which the behaviour occurs.
....
....

What actually occurs?
....
....

Who else is involved ? Is it the same people ?
....
....

Does this behaviour occur in many different contexts?
....
....

Is there a common sequence of events of pattern of interactions that usually takes place? Describe exactly what happens. (What is the normal sequence of events? Who does what where and when? What is the result, and so on.)
....
....
....
....
....

Can the student control or significantly delay the undesirable behaviour under certain circumstances or is the undesirable behaviour almost always present?
....
....

Is the undesirable behaviour generally a response to someone or to something that has just happened?
....
....

2. Conduct a private talk

Meet when you're both calm

You need to meet when both of you have calmed down. Never attempt to have a discussion with a student who is still angry, or when you are still angry. Find a location where you can be observed but not overheard by other people to abide by student protection legislation. Speak in a quiet voice and give the student some physical space. It is often helpful to "walk and talk". Suggest that you go for a walk around the football field or around the playground: side-by-side is often easier than face-to-face for both in these situations.

Thank the student

Thank the student for agreeing to meet. Remember he has chosen to meet with you. If he *really* didn't want to, he wouldn't be there. Acknowledge that he probably would rather be doing other things.

Take a shared problem approach

"We've got a problem in class, Jarrod, and we need to work out a way to solve it." Avoid using the word "you" in a series of statements like "You keep disrupting the class", or "You're always talking and distracting other people". The situation is a problem for both of you and both of you need to co-operate to sort it out.

Focus on behaviour

Focus on the behaviour and its effects. Problem behaviour should be recognised as just that - problem behaviour. It must never be suggested that it is the student that is the problem - the problem is the behaviour.

Acknowledge student's point of view

Acknowledge the student's point of view but try to direct the conversation to a solution. Using expressions like "I appreciate that....", "I can see that....", "I recognise...", "I acknowledge....", "I accept that...." helps the student realise that his point of view is being received and deflects some of the hostility the student may be experiencing.

Identify positive student behaviours

Identify features of the student's behaviour that are good. Refer to some occasion when the student was doing the right thing and how well it worked. (You may believe that these occasions do not exist, but you can usually find one occasion to draw on!) It's important that the student sees himself as being capable of success. "Remember when you did that project with Paul? That turned out really well" or "Remember early in the year when you were trying really hard? Your work was going well then." Try to identify with the student what was happening on that occasion that made it successful. Was it the people he was working with? Was it that he just liked that topic? Did he find that work easy, but it's too hard now?

Don't ask 'Why?'

It is usually not helpful to ask a student *why* he did something. Often students are not aware themselves of the complex reasons behind their behaviours. It is usually more productive to discuss *what happened*, and what rules or rights the behaviour interfered with.

Invite co-operation in making a plan

You need to invite the student's co-operation in planning some alternative. This continues the "shared problem" approach.

Clarify the plan

Different alternatives are explored later in this chapter. If no plan emerges from the meeting, you have still given the student the message that you consider him important enough to spend time on. That message alone is important for students who may be struggling with their place in the class.

Remind about agreed action

If you do come up with a plan or alternative, ensure that, before you part, the student knows what the next step in implementing the plan will be. Remind the student at the end of the talk about the agreed action.

Thank student for co-operation

Thank him for spending the time working on a plan. Stress the fact that you believe in his ability to accomplish the task. It is important to build a student's self esteem and confidence by adopting a positive outlook.

Express confidence in student

Conclude the meeting by saying something like, "I have confidence that we can work this out. I'm going to try and I know you are going to try". This is better than a reminder of the punishments that will befall the student if his behaviour doesn't improve.

3. Set up a private cueing system

One plan that you may suggest is the establishment of a private cueing system. Sometimes when a student is constantly off task, out of his seat, or otherwise distracted, it is a good idea to try to help the child become aware of when he is wasting time. In your private talk with him, suggest that you and he develop a secret signal (or *private* signal for secondary students) that will indicate that he is "off task" and needs to get back "on task".

Explain the "secret signal"

No-one else in the class will know what the signal means, but for the student concerned, it will be a silent sign that he needs to stop wasting time and get back to work.

Just about anything can be incorporated into this strategy. Try to get the student to come up with a suggestion. Perhaps placing a pencil into a coffee mug on your desk will be the signal. If you doubt that the student would be aware enough to check your desk, you may set up a signal on his desk. You may walk past and move something on his desk into another position. You might have a small object that you place on his desk as you move past.

Rehearse student response to cue

Once you and the student agree on the signal, rehearse the meaning of the cue with him. Pick up the small object and say, "When I put this on your desk, what am I trying to tell you? What do you need to do?"

Change cue when necessary

These strategies generally work for a short time because of their novelty value. Don't become discouraged if you need to change the cueing system regularly in order to keep the student motivated. You are still helping the student become aware of his behaviour, which is the first step in helping him change it.

4. Use timers to monitor behaviour

Another more public strategy is to use auditory signals to help the student monitor his behaviour. Tape a series of "beeps" at different intervals on a 30 minute audio tape. The beeps may come at two minutes, five minutes, seven minutes, ten minutes, and so on. The tape recorder is placed where the student will be able to hear it but where it will not be too distracting. Turn the player on when seatwork begins. Each time the beep is heard, the student checks if he is on task. If he isn't, the beep is a reminder to return to his task.

5. Set up a monitoring program

Another strategy you may discuss in your private talk is a self-monitoring program. This is another, more advanced strategy for helping students become aware of their behaviour. There are several important steps in setting up such a program.

Select target behaviours

You need to help the student identify a particular behaviour that is causing difficulty and an alternative to that behaviour. In the past, it was believed that mentioning a negative behaviour might be counterproductive, however, both ends of the continuum lack a reference point unless you combine them into a dual focus in prevention. By taking this dual focus approach, the student becomes aware of what he shouldn't be doing, but also of what he should be doing. This allows the teacher and the student to monitor both the frequency of unwanted behaviour and the frequency of target behaviours; for example, "Jarrod, I need you to stop leaving your desk (unwanted behaviour) and finish your assigned work (target behaviour)".

Monitor target behaviours

It is important that the student tries to take control of his behaviour rather than have the behaviour managed by the teacher. The first step in assisting a student manage his own behaviour involves developing his awareness of the frequency of the unwanted behaviour. The purpose of asking the student to monitor the negative behaviours and then to start recording the number of times a target behaviour has taken place, is to assist him to develop a self-monitoring approach.

Provide the student with a check list of positive and negative behaviours (see Box 7.2). The student puts a tick whenever he recognises the fact that a behaviour has occurred. This can be done in conjunction with the taped reminders described above. Do it over a single period or lesson at first. If the student can self monitor and can identify target and problem behaviours, there is a good chance that he will be able manage a behaviour change.

Box 7.2 Behaviour Monitor

Target behaviour		**Unwanted behaviour**	
I put up my hand		I called out	
I stayed in my seat		I got out of my seat	
I completed my work		I did not finish my work	

Compare notes

The teacher also completes a checklist and the two can compare their perceptions at the end of the lesson. This comparison assists the student to identify the times when he was in the wrong place or doing the wrong thing as well as identifying more precisely the desired behaviours.

Self-recording is a valuable tool in behaviour change as the mere fact of self-monitoring can lead to behaviour change. In many situations the student produces unwanted behaviours without really being aware of it. The behaviour has become so automatic that it is almost outside his conscious awareness. For this reason monitoring promotes changes in behaviour as the focus is directed towards desired and undesired behaviours.

6. Rehearse target behaviours

Model behaviour

With younger children, you should actually rehearse the desired behaviours. You take the role of the student, sit in the desk and put up your hand to demonstrate what to do requesting help. This is referred to as modelling and it gives the student a clear understanding of what is expected. Once the student knows what is expected the teacher should ask the student to rehearse the behaviour whilst pretending that the class lesson is in progress.

7. Shape desired behaviours using encouragement

It is important to do more than simply tell a student when he is doing the wrong thing. You need to provide statements that both encourage the student and that clearly shape a preferred behaviour. In shaping and encouraging behaviour there are three important components of the statements you will use.

Identify desired behaviour

Identify the desired behaviour in situations where it would have been appropriate, but where the student has behaved inappropriately.

Identify past successes

Identify a past incident that was handled successfully and remind him that he has acted sensibly, maturely, and appropriately at an earlier time.

Express confidence

Express confidence in his ability to exhibit appropriate behaviour.

Usually a number of encouraging statements are linked together. You state the desired behaviour; remind the student that he is able to do the correct thing; and express confidence that the student can do it. Give reasons that support your belief in the student. These can be tied to a recognition of ability ("you are a sensible student"), or past evidence ("you've been able to do [target behaviour] before"). The statement should end with further encouragement such as "You can do it" or "I know how you will try to make it work". Some examples of such statements appear in Box 7.3

Box 7.3 Examples of Encouraging Statements to Shape Behaviour

> "Jarrod, it's important to stay in your seat and finish your work. I know you can because last week you finished everything on time."
>
> "I know you can handle the situation... you have been able to work out similar problems before. Remember last week when you..."
>
> "You can do it.... You are very good at sorting out lots of these kinds of ... and I have faith in you."

Praise as soon as behaviour begins

Shaping behaviour is a process that starts when the student commences (not completes) a requested behaviour. Recognise effort. Don't wait until the set task has been completed before making an encouraging statement. When shaping a behaviour, it is vital to indicate to the student that you are pleased that he has started the task.

You need to ensure that students hear positive messages as you shape new behaviours. Key statements such as "I have confidence in you ..." and "I like the way you handled that situation ... etc" should occur very frequently.

8. Draw up a Contract

Contracts between you and an individual student can be a useful aid to changing more disruptive behaviour. A contract sets up more formalised structures to support an agreement you may have reached in your private talk.

It is important to identify exactly what the behaviour was that caused the problem. The contract could be completed together with the teacher providing as much guidance as necessary, while remaining non-judgmental. The agreed-upon behaviours, such as staying in seat or not calling out, are specifically listed. It may be that the student will agree to the behaviours only for a short period of time, for example, ten minutes per lesson or session. If this is all you can get, go with it! It may in fact be quite a difficult task for the student concerned. A sample of an individual contract appears in Box 7.4 on the following page.

Make the contract for a short period of time, between a week and a month. Revise the contract at the end of each day at the beginning of the contract period. If two days go by without the target behaviours being met, you will need to revise the contract.

You may need to combine the program with a cueing system to help him monitor his behaviour. An incentive program which rewards the students for small gains should also be used in conjunction with the contract.

Box 7.4 Sample Contract

Name: .... Class: ....

What I did
....
....

What I could have done instead
....
....

What I will do next time
....
....

How this is better
....
....

Who or what will help me do this?
....
....

Signed   ....   (Student)
Signed   ....   (Teacher)
Date   ....

Date for next discussion ....

Final Note

As with all techniques, these strategies are useful only if the student is willing to try to change his behaviour. This is much more likely to happen if the student believes that you like him and genuinely want to help him.

The power of the personal relationship that you develop with your students cannot be underestimated. As we mentioned in a previous chapter, easily distracted students, such as those with ADHD or Asperger's, need the motivation of a strong personal connection with their teacher to help them stay focused and on-task.

Students with oppositional or conduct disorders need the strength of that personal relationship even more. These students cause the most disruptive behaviour in schools. Many of them believe that no-one likes them or cares what happens to them. In some schools, this almost seems to be true. If you can convince the student that you believe he is worth helping, and that you really want to help him, you may be able to turn that student's life around.

Chapter 8

MANAGING YOUR OWN RESPONSES

Introduction

We have talked at length in this book about the importance of recognising individual differences in your classes. These differences invariably mean that you will at some stage be confronted by situations in which some children behave in very unexpected ways. Children who experience difficulty in sustaining or focusing attention, who may be excessively active, who are defiant, or very hard to manage in other ways, will often test you and your value system more than any other aspect of educational endeavour.

Teachers are understandably anxious about being given a "difficult" class. Having hard to manage children in the class is regarded as one of the most stressful aspects of teaching. You will probably all have vivid memories of having difficult classes (probably on Friday afternoons) during teaching practice. We certainly do! With essays on Piaget or Vygotsky clearly in our mind, brimming with knowledge and ready to give the children the benefit of our newly acquired wisdom, we entered classrooms full of enthusiasm, but somehow the students just weren't interested in what we had prepared. Those greatly anticipated, alert and smiling students with eyes and minds ablaze with the joy of learning did not materialise. Somehow all those lesson plans, History of Education lectures, pedagogy and Piaget had not prepared us for a difficult class on a Friday afternoon.

How easy it is under those circumstances to fall into the trap of dreading that class again the following week. We wanted a "better" class (which by deduction means that the first was a "bad" class). If we had had heart monitors and skin conductance measures strapped to us during the day, there would have been no doubt that dangerously high heart beats and high levels of tension would have been recorded as we approached the time of the day when that difficult class had to be faced again.

> The real voyage of discovery consists not in seeking new landscapes but in having new eyes.
> *Marcel Proust*

It is very easy to start thinking thoughts like:
> "I'll never cope... its going to be awful. The kids must know that I'm not sure if I can handle them.... I am beginning to wonder if I can make it as a teacher if I can't handle my first difficult class.... Maybe next week I'll have a sickie....".

Clearly these thoughts are not particularly helpful - in fact they're counter-productive. At this point the teacher is experiencing a considerable amount of what can only be described as stress.

Stress

Stress comes in response to situations that are perceived to be difficult or threatening (Sarafino, 1998). If ten different teachers were given the same difficult class, not all would become stressed or distressed. It might be that three teachers would feel varying levels of discomfort or stress but the other seven teachers would generally cope quite well and not show a stress reaction. Why do seven out of ten show almost no concerns but three teachers experience elevated levels of stress?

The explanation again comes down to individual differences and the fact that each individual teacher assesses the situation differently. Difficult situations themselves do not produce stress. It is the way that each person views the situation that primarily decides how the stressful situation is to be handled. A long time ago a Greek philosopher call Heraclitus stated that:

> **It is not the events that so disturb us, it is the view which we take of them.**

In other words, the degree to which a stressful situation has the potential to affect us is the degree to which we allow it (Lazarus & Folkman, 1984). There is no doubt that some classes and some children are more difficult than others, but our emotional reaction is determined to a considerable degree by the "views that we take" of the situation. So if we look closely at our appraisal of the situation, we may begin to recognise that our thinking plays a role in determining our interpretation of the stressful events. The meaning that we place on an event influences our emotional reaction and our coping skills (Lazarus & Folkman, 1984).

> **Event/Situation → Appraisal → Our Reaction**

Imagine that one day a student refuses to do something and an argument develops. The situation escalates and the student then runs out of the room. Your appraisal may go something like this:

> "This is a disaster. I am a failure if I can't get a 9 year old to do something. Now the rest of the class will be even harder to control because they have seen that I can't make Tracey do what she was told. I bet they tell all the other kids and their parents and everyone will know that I am having a problem in the classroom. Before long I'll have the principal here. I should have been able to resolve the problem without getting to this stage. I've failed completely as a manager."

If this cycle repeats itself often enough, eventually you *will be* convinced that you *are* a hopeless teacher. Perhaps you may even blame Tracey and decide that she is a "problem" child. Clearly such a belief may have a considerable impact on your relationship with this student. When students are difficult to manage, especially in public places such as classrooms, the impact of their behaviour on teachers can be quite significant. You may feel embarrassed, lose confidence, become discouraged and eventually feel defeated as a teacher. Once unhelpful thinking becomes established, it doesn't take long for it to accumulate and create stress.

Reactions to Stress

One of the pioneers of stress research (Selye, 1985) indicated that there are three stages through which we can go in relation to stress.

Alarm reaction

In this stage we react quickly because we are perceiving the stressor as threatening. Our reaction is referred to as a 'Fight or Flight' response. We experience adrenalin-related changes where we can see events as a threat and our body reacts by preparing us for perceived problems.

Resistance

In this stage our bodies manage the stress. We may be constantly experiencing stress and even habituate to it, but our body keeps score. The stress may be affecting our health in very subtle ways which are at first difficult to detect because the symptoms are well hidden (for example, elevated blood pressure, tension, etc).

Exhaustion

In this stage we are becoming " burnt out" and we may experience a range of problems. It is now quite apparent that the body and the mind are experiencing stress as the indicators are no longer as covert as they were in the resistance stage. We succumb to a range of disorders like headaches, tiredness, sleep disorders, worry and anxiety. In more stressful situations our immune system functions less well and we become sick.

You should recognise that the thinker in the previous example had really let the situation overwhelm him and one incident had grown out of all proportion. An unpleasant situation was being regarded as an absolute catastrophe!

> Everything can be taken from us but one thing, which is the last of the human freedoms – to choose one's attitude in any given set of circumstances, to choose one's own way. *Victor Frankl, Holocaust survivor*

How stress affects your thinking

Unhelpful thinking has certain words or phrases that accompany it. These words or phrases are like strong glue that makes unhelpful thinking difficult to change. Beck (1976) has introduced the idea that individuals continually evaluate themselves in relation to their performances and to other people's opinions of themselves. This stream of inferences Beck has called automatic thoughts. These thoughts become so much a part of our everyday language and experience that we stop being aware of them. This thinking becomes *automatic*. Words and ideas pop into our heads without any invitation or effort on our part, and they bring with them feelings of unhappiness, anger, frustration, helplessness, and so forth. These thoughts are linked to our way of seeing the world and to previous similar experiences.

There are certain patterns of maladaptive beliefs in automatic thoughts. These thoughts can be given labels that describe the general tenor of their content. Following is a discussion of the various themes that appear in automatic thoughts which develop under stressful situations.

Catastrophisation/Magnification

If something does not work out, it is considered "a total catastrophe". Recovery from this is deemed impossible. It is a huge setback. If you catastrophise, you lose perspective and magnify it until it is not just a problem but an absolute catastrophe.

> "This is a disaster. I can't handle it."
> "I don't believe how hard this class is. I'll never manage them."
> This is an absolutely *No Win* Situation !"

Overgeneralisation

You make wide and sweeping judgments on the basis of one piece of evidence. Judgments are completely black or white. You may also draw oversimplified or generalised conclusions on the basis of inadequate, incomplete or superficial evidence

> "*Everything* I do goes wrong"
> "I failed before therefore *I'll never get it right.*"

"I tried it once (some kind of classroom management approach) and it didn't work then so it will never work."

Selective Attending

You focus on the negative aspects of the experience and all others are either discounted or merge into the background. You fail to notice any positive aspects. It is like wearing some kind of contact lens that prevents pleasant events being recorded and only recognises problems and negative events.

"She is so difficult to manage. She was an absolute horror today. She pushed Bethany over, and ... " (The fact is that for most of the day the student in question was fine but for five minutes a problem emerged.)

> Every thought you have makes up some segment of the world you see. It is with your thought, then that we must work, if your perception of the world is to be changed. A Course in Miracles

"Should" Statements

You believe that there are universal "shoulds" which have to occur so that you can be happy.

"I *should* get support from the school executive ...."
"They *should* do something about those boys."

"Need" Statements

These statements are often used with "should" statements, but may be used alone. In order to be happy, contented, or successful, you believe that something is essential. Often individuals fail to distinguish between needs and wants.

"I just *needed* a quiet day and they started being difficult
"I know they do it deliberately ... I just *needed* them to behave - they didn't and it was awful."

Mind Reading

As part of the catastrophisation process, you believe that someone else is thinking negatively about you. Mind reading occurs when you attribute to others (without any evidence) a set of beliefs.

> "*I know* that the kids behave like this on purpose."
> "*They deliberately do it* to annoy me"
> "*I know that the principal thinks* I'm a hopeless teacher after she saw me with Danny and Paul ... they just wouldn't behave."

Perfectionism and "All or Nothing" Thinking

The setting of impossibly high standards is termed perfectionism. Everyone is imperfect, everyone makes mistakes but your expectation is that you must succeed in order to be worthwhile. Such a belief causes undue suffering because it is invariably linked with self or other blame and "all or nothing" thinking.

> "Either I get all the class to behave properly all the time or I must be a bad teacher (or they are a ' bad class'.) "
> "That was hopeless. I should have completed the program today and we only got half way... that was a disaster."

In "all or nothing" scenarios, individuals take an extreme position (like perfectionism) where everything is either black or white. Either everyone loves me or no-one cares. Either I get at least a distinction or I am a failure.

Permanently Set in Concrete

When you catastrophise, you can make something that is temporary (e.g. feeling sad, angry, frustrated) into something permanent - forever! The whole situation overwhelms you and you feel that things will never improve.

Self Blame

Sometimes you can become extremely negative about yourself. You judge yourself too harshly when you have failed to overcome some obstacle or problem. The effect of such harsh criticism and judgments is to condemn yourself for making a wrong decision or failing to do something correctly.

> "I must be weak, inadequate, hopeless etc."

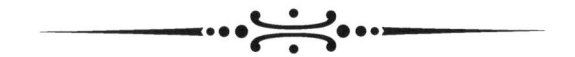

When you're under stress, you can combine any of the above responses into a long diatribe against yourself that convinces you that you will never make the grade as a teacher. Notice how many of the categories of unhelpful thoughts often run into each other in the three examples below.

> "I should have remembered to do that ... and because I didn't that means I'm just hopeless (perfectionism). I should have known that she was going to react like that and blow up (note the "should") and I should have been prepared. Then the principal had to come in and that was awful (note the catastrophising). I bet he thought what a hopeless teacher I must be (mind reading)."

> "She is so difficult to manage. She was an absolute horror today. She pushed Bethany over. ...and I just needed a quiet day and they just started being difficult (need statement). I know they do it deliberately (mind reading). I just needed them to behave - they didn't and it was awful about those boys. Its hopeless - a total disaster! (catastrophising)"

> "I'll never cope with her (overgeneralisation). She is turning into a little monster and I just can't cope. I am hopeless (catastrophisation). I'll never be able to manage her properly (overgeneralisation). I should never have had started teaching in this school or even teaching anywhere. She's uncontrollable and I'm just a disaster at managing difficult situations (catastrophisation). What's the point of bothering. Its always going to be like this.... it'll never change (set in concrete)!! "

The tyranny of what you believe!

In the above thought scenario there is a great deal of catastrophising. At the end of the day, the teacher's negative thinking has resulted in a great deal of self blame, failure statements and "shoulds". The overall tenor of these automatic thoughts is negative and self-critical. Thoughts of this nature are setting up the teacher for some level of depression. It's easy to reflect with hindsight that some things should have been handled more effectively. Unfortunately, life is lived in a forward direction and you don't have the luxury of a crystal ball.

In order to address the problems that occur as a result of negative thinking, it is important to become aware of how we respond to problem situations.

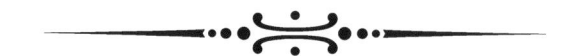

Changing your Automatic Thoughts

The process of learning to be more positive, to develop better coping skills and to reduce stress requires you to:

- Monitor your automatic thoughts.
- Recognize the connections between these thoughts, moods and behaviour.
- Examine the evidence for and against your negative automatic thoughts.
- Challenge the negative thoughts and substitute adaptive coping self statements (Beck et al, 1990).

How can we change our unhelpful thoughts?

> What lies behind us, and what lies before us are tiny matters compared to what lies within us.
> Ralph Waldo Emerson

Just for a moment let's recall the teacher's comments that were made in the earlier passage. Instead of examining them in relation to an internal dialogue, let's consider that you said them to a friend who is teaching on the same staff. She has just had a fairly difficult time with a particular boy.

> "You'll *never* cope with her ... she is turning into a little monster and its clear that you *just can't cope. I think its pretty hopeless. You'll never be able to manage her* properly... maybe you *should* never have had started teaching in this school (or even teaching anywhere) ... *she's uncontrollable and you seem to be just a disaster at managing difficult situations*. What's the point of bothering ... its always going to be like this .... *it'll never change!!*"

You would never speak to a friend in this manner. You are supportive and encouraging with friends if they are having a hard time, but you tend to be much harder on yourself. Rather then choose thoughts that are positive and helpful you may let negative and depressive ideas fill your mind. You need to be "supportive and encouraging" to yourself.

The above comments dramatise the way that you can be negative to yourself. If you talked like that to your friends, you would soon be friendless. But often that is how you speak to your own inner self. You need to stop being over-critical of your own failings and start to understand how to counteract your own negative self talk.

Learning to 'dispute' negative thoughts (Changing negatives into positives)

Once you are aware of the types of negative or maladaptive thinking that occur, it is vital to deactivate these thoughts and change them into more positive, coping statements. There are a number of approaches that you can use when automatic negative thinking emerges (Salkovskis, 1996).

Ask: Where is the evidence?

This needs to be one of the first thoughts that come to mind as it is very valuable. It is applied to a belief that needs to be checked against reality. Use such questions as:

"Where is the evidence for that?"
"What proof do I have that?"
"How does it follow that... ?"

Challenge mind reading

When you engage in mind reading, you are assuming that you know what another person is thinking and then react accordingly. You treat your opinion, suspicions and even fear as if it were based on fact. If the principal or another teacher comments about the class being noisy on Wednesday afternoon, you assume they are thinking that you are a hopeless teacher. You need to challenge this type of mind-reading with evidence based questions such as those referred to above:

"Where is the evidence for my belief?"
"What proof do I have that they are having a dig at me?"
"Maybe they were suggesting we were having a good time."

Seek alternative interpretations

Sometimes you can draw conclusions about an event that are less probable than a number of other possibilities. For example, if you came out to the car park and saw that one of your tyres was flat you might draw the conclusion that " one of the boys in my class has done this!" A more logical and plausible alternative explanation is that you had a small puncture from running over a nail on the way to school and the tyre has lost air throughout the day. This is an example of a challenge to the automatic thought that was fairly confrontational and negative.

Don't accept as fact the first thought or idea that pops into your head. Challenge it to see if there are alternative ways to view the events or situation. What might other people suggest are possible explanations for what has happened?

Rate the Catastrophe

Sometimes events occur which are not particularly desirable but you may massively overreact to these situations. Think about rating a world disaster on a scale of 1 to 10, with 1 being no problem and 10 meaning a disaster of enormous magnitude. If you rate teaching a difficult class at 8-9 and a very difficult student in your class as a 10, then you really are catastrophising. It is essential to check any tendency to catastrophise by asking ourselves:

"Is this really as bad as I'm making out?"
"It's not like this is a matter of life or death"
"It may not be nice but it's not the end of the world"
"What is so awful about this that means I couldn't cope?"

It is important to keep perspective!

Challenge "All or Nothing" Thinking and Perfectionism

Sometimes called "Black and White thinking", "all or nothing" thinking takes the view that everything must work perfectly or it is a total disaster. Clearly such extreme thinking places you and the students in your class in a very difficult position. More productive thoughts to apply to yourself or to your class are:

"OK, you weren't 100% successful, in fact, only about 40%, but that doesn't mean you're a total failure."
"A journey of 100 miles requires a first step. There is a long way to go but at least I'm further ahead than I was before I started."
"At the time I made the best decision I could. Perhaps in hindsight I'd have done something different but at the time that decision seemed correct."

> The most powerful thing you can do to change the world is to change your beliefs about the nature of life, people, reality to something more positive and begin to act accordingly. Shakti Gawain

Take another's view

You often lose focus when you remain within your own thoughts. Try to imagine yourself as the friend of someone having a few problems. In that case, you would be unlikely to say to them:

> "Well this proves that you are pretty hopeless at classroom management. You really shouldn't be teaching if you can't manage a few difficult 9-10 year olds."

We would be more likely to say:

> "Hey come on, don't lose perspective over this. The kids are a bit difficult sure, but you are doing really well. Don't forget that for most of the day they are reasonably well behaved and it's only sometimes that they are a real challenge. There are lots of teachers all over the country who have difficult classes and they aren't "beating themselves up". You're really good at lots of things but at the moment you're letting this get to you. Don't feel like you have to succeed at everything. Some things take time and anyway you said yourself there are some good days when the kids behave quite well for a reasonable part of the day. Don't just focus on what goes wrong. Try to remember all the times that they are working well and behaviour isn't a problem. You can handle it. I know that you can so don't let it get to you! Stop beating yourself up and look at what you have done with these kids!"

Very often people will apply one standard to themselves (harsh) and another (less judgmental) to others. Most people forgive others – and don't expect standards of perfectionism. Most people don't condemn people for making mistakes. Learn to forgive yourself! You can often overestimate your own level of responsibility. If you do this, your confidence and your self esteem will be affected and you are likely to be less effective in the classroom.

> Life is not the way it should be ... it's the way it is and its how we cope that makes the difference. *Virginia Satir*

Challenge "Should" and "Need" Thoughts

Once you start to say things such as "I need X or Y to be happy" and "Someone should" do something, you immediately set yourself up for potential disappointment. When we use such forceful words as "I *need* this" and "It *should* have happened", we are creating an all or nothing situation.

Life almost never goes according to plan. Life should be fair, but quite often is not. We deserve that job, but somebody else gets it. Students should be better behaved, but often they're not. If you distress yourself all the time about what "should" be in comparison to what "is" you will have a disappointing journey through life.

Positive self-talk requires practice

The process of disputing or challenging negative beliefs or attributions does not come automatically and requires practice and awareness of our internal self-talk. It is important to "talk sense to ourselves" and recognise the importance of maintaining a clear perspective and not catastrophising, selectively attending or using "all or nothing" thinking (Wragg, 1989).

One way that we can become aware of automatic thoughts that arise in the face of difficult and challenging situations in the classroom is to keep a record of the automatic thoughts as they appear. In order to promote awareness of the process of analysing our self-talk and challenging the degree to which it is catastrophic or problematic the suggested outline below could be used.

Box 8.1 Analysing and Challenging Thoughts

Situation	Automatic thoughts	Challenges to automatic thoughts

- In the first column identify a recent situation that you believed wasn't managed well.
- In the second column try to remember what your automatic thoughts were. Identify how the thoughts impacted upon your feelings and try to decide if you behaved in a way that was helpful or unhelpful. If you found yourself thinking negative thoughts about a difficult child or class or even your own ability to manage the situation, then it is important to see if your style of thinking fits into any of the unhelpful or negative thinking errors that are likely to produce a stress reaction. If negative thoughts are occurring, it is important to dispute them and replace them with more positive, helpful thoughts.
- In the third column, dispute or challenge the negative thoughts using the strategies outlined above.

> It is not the events themselves that disturb us it is the view which we take of them. *Heraclitus*

Keeping a Challenges Diary

It is important to systematically attack and dispute these negative thoughts. In order to discover what works for you, a Challenges Diary could be kept. Remember you will have some good days, and some bad ones. Don't expect your irrational beliefs to disappear completely. You must expect some bad days to avoid discouragement.

1. Keep a record of all the challenges you find effective in reducing anxiety or other negative emotions.
2. For each challenge, record on a series of 10 - point scales:
   - the strength of the emotion before challenging
   - the strength of the challenging
   - how long the challenge was used, and
   - the strength of the emotion after challenging.

3. The best challenges are those which remove a negative emotion when it is quite strong. You should be particularly careful to keep accurate records on those challenges that remove or reduce anxiety attacks or severe depressive episodes.
4. After a sufficient number of workable challenges has been gathered, select those which produced the greatest reductions in negative emotions. Next, develop a new series of challenges emphasizing the key points in previously successful challenges.
5. Continue to refine these challenges, based on trial and error. Eventually you will develop some very powerful, effective strategies.

This type of stress management aims to deactivate the negative thinking. The negative thoughts will not necessarily stop, but you will have developed some successful strategies to challenge negative, harmful, stress-inducing thoughts, and replaced them with thoughts that are more realistic and helpful.

> As a man thinks so does he become. Every man is the son of his own works.
> Cervantes

REFERENCES

Adler, A. (1957). *Understanding human nature*. New York: Fawcett.

Allinder, R.M. (1994). The relationship between efficacy and the instructional practices of special education teachers and consultants. *Teacher Education and Special Education, 17*(2), 86-95.

American Psychiatric Association. (1968). *Diagnostic and statistical manual of mental disorders*. Washington, DC: Author.

American Psychiatric Association. (1994). *Diagnostic and statistical manual of mental disorders*. (4th ed.). Washington, DC: Author.

Andrews, R.J., Elkins, J., Berry, P.B. & Burge, J.A. (1979). *A survey of special education in Australia: Provisions, needs and priorities in the education of children with handicaps and learning difficulties*. St Lucia, Queensland: Fred and Eleanor Schonell Educational Research Centre.

Anastopoulos, A. & Barkley, R.A. (1992). Attention deficit-hyperactivity disorder. In E.C. Walker & M.C. Roberts (Eds.), *Handbook of clinical child psychology* (pp.413-430). Canada: John Wiley & Sons.

Askew, B.L. (1993). *Practices of special education teachers for dealing with students with ADD/ADHD*. Unpublished Masters, St Xavier University, Chicago, Illinois.

Attwood, T. (1998). *Asperger's Syndrome: A guide for parents and professionals*. London: Jessica Kingsley Publishers.

August, G.J. & Garfinkel, B.D. (1990). Comorbidity of ADHD and reading disability among client-referred children. *Journal of Abnormal Child Psychology, 18*(1), 29-45.

Bailey, J. & Rice, D. (Eds.). (1997). *Attention Deficit/Hyperactivity Disorder: Medical, psychological and educational perspectives*. Sefton, NSW: Robert Burton Printers.

Balson, M. (1995). *Understanding classroom behaviour*. (4th Ed.), Melbourne: ACER.

Barkley, R.A. (1987). *Defiant children*. New York: Guildford Press.

Barkley, R.A. (1990). *Attention Deficit Hyperactivity Disorder: A handbook for diagnosis and treatment*. New York: Guildford Press.

Barkley, R.A. (2001). A theory of ADHD: Inhibitions, self-control, and time. Proceedings of the conference of the *Children's Hospital Education Research Institute*, Westmead, March 16-19, pp.12-16.

Basch, M.F. (1989). The teacher, the transference and development. In K. Field, Cohler, B. & Wool, G. (Eds.), *Learning and education: Psychoanalytic perspectives* (pp.771-787). Madison, CN: International Universities, Inc.

Batton, M. & Russell, J. (1995). *Students at risk: a review of Australian literature 1980-1994.* Melbourne: ACER.

Bauer, M.S. & Balius, F.A. Jr. (1995). Storytelling: Integrating therapy and curriculum for students with serious emotional disturbances. *Teaching Exceptional Children, 27*(2) 24-28.

Baumrind, D. (1986). New directions in socialization research. *American Psychologist, 35,* 639-652.

Beane, A.L. (1999). *The bully-free classroom: Over 100 tips and strategies for teachers K-8.* Minneapolis: Free Spirit Publishing Inc.

Beck, A.T. (1976). *Cognitive therapy and emotional disorders.* Philadelphia: University of Pennsylvania Press.

Beck, M., Springer, K., Beachy, L., Hoger, M. & Buddey, L. (1990). The losing formula. *Newsweek,* pp.52-58.

Bender, W.N. & Mathes, M.Y. (1995). Students with ADHD in the inclusive classroom: A hierarchical approach to strategy selection. *Intervention in School and Clinic, 30*(4), 226-234.

Bernstein, N. (1996). *Treating the unmanageable adolescent: A guide to oppositional defiant and conduct disorders.* New Jersey, Book-Mart Press.

Bradley, D., Bjorlykke, L., Mann, E., Homon, C. & Lindsay, J. (1993). *Empowerment of the general educator through effective teaching strategies.* John Hopkins University.

Bronfenbrenner, U. (1979). *The ecology of human development: Experiments by nature and design.* Cambridge, MA: Harvard University Press.

Carlson, C., Tamm, L. & Gaub, M. (1997). Gender differences in children with ADHD, ODD and co-occurring ADHD/ODD identified in a school population. *Journal of the American Academy of Child and Adolescent Psychiatry, 36*(12), 1709-1711.

Cannon, G.S., Idol, L. & West, J.F. (1992). Educating students with mild handicaps in general classrooms: Essential teaching practices for general and special educators. *Journal of Learning Disabilities, 25*(5), 300-317.

Canter, L. & Canter M. (1976). *Assertive discipline – A take charge approach for today's educator.* Santa Monica, CA: Canter.

Canter, L. (1990). Assertive Discipline. In Scherer, Gersch & Fry (Eds.) *Meeting disruptive behaviour: Assessment, intervention and partnership,* London: Macmillan.

Carey, W.B. & MacDevitt, S.C. (1978). The importance of temperament and environment interaction. In M.E. Lewis & L.A. Rosenblum (Eds.), *Control of human behaviour* (vol. 3, pp.86-96) Glenview, IL:

Carmichael, P., Adkins, Gaal, I., Hutchins, P., Levy, F., McCormack, J., Oberklaid, F., Pearson, C. & Storm, V. (1997). *Attention Deficit Hyperactivity Disorder*: National Health and Medical Research Council.

Carroll, A. (1993). Current perspectives on attention deficit hyperactivity disorder: A review of the literature. *Australasian Journal of Special Education, 18*(1), 15-24.

Chess, S. & Thomas, A. (1984). *Origins and evolutions of behavior disorders.* New York: Bruner/Mazel.

Christenson, S.L., Thurlow, M.L. & Ysseldyke, J.E. (1987). *Instructional effectiveness: Implications for effective instruction of handicapped students.* Washington, DC: Office of Special Education and Rehabilitative Services.

Clements, S. & Peters, J. (1962). *Minimal brain dysfunction in children: Terminology and justification* (Public Health Service Publication No. 1415). Washington, DC: Department of Health, Education and Welfare.

Coleman, M. (1986). *Behaviour disorders: Theory and practice.* New Jersey: Prentice Hall.

Connell, H.M., Irvine, L. & Rodney, J. (1982). Psychiatric disorder in Queensland primary school children. *Australian Paediatric Journal, 18,* 177-188.

Cooper, P. & Ideus, K. (1995). Is attention deficit hyperactivity disorder a Trojan Horse? *Support for Learning, 10*(1), 31-39.

Crocker, R. (1986). *What research says to the teacher: Classroom processes and student outcomes.* Paper presented at the Conference of the Canadian Society for the Study of Education, Winnipeg, Manitoba, Canada.

Cumine, V., Leach, J. & Stevenson, G. (1998). *Asperger Syndrome.* London: David Fulton Publishers Ltd.

Dinkmeyer, D.C., McKay, G.D. & Dinkmeyer, D. Jnr. (1980). *Systematic training for effective teaching.* Circle Pines, MN: American Guidance Service.

Dreikurs, R. (1968). *Psychology in the classroom* (2nd Ed.). New York: Harper & Row.

Dreikurs, R. & Cassell, P. (1972). *Discipline without tears.* New York: Hawthorn.

Dreikurs, R., Grunwald, B. & Pepper, F. (1982). *Maintaining sanity in the classroom.* New York: Harper & Row.

Dunlap, D.M., Gleason, M. & Waugh, R. (1982). Aiming at excellence: A comparison of the school effectiveness literature and special education practice. *Oregon School Study Council Bulletin, 25*(10), 1-40.

Edwards, G.H. & Barkley, R.A. (1997). Attention deficit/hyperactivity disorder: History, diagnosis and current concepts. In J. Bailey & D. Rice (Eds.), *Attention deficit/hyperactivity disorder: Medical, psychological and educational perspectives* (pp.1-18). Sefton, NSW: The Australian Association of Special Education.

Ehlers, S. & Gillberg, C. (1993). The epidemiology of Asperger Syndrome: a total population study. *Journal of Child Psychology and Psychiatry, 34,* 1327-1350.

Ellard, J. (1993). Attention deficit disorder: An introductory note. *Modern Medicine, 26*(1), 3-5.

Ellis, E.S., Worthington, L.A. & Larkin, M.J. (1994). *Research synthesis on effective teaching principles and the design of quality tools for educators.* (Technical Report No. 6): University of Oregon.

Elton Report (1989). *A report on school behaviour and discipline.* London, UK: Government Inspectorate.

Englert, C. (1984). Measuring teacher effectiveness from the teacher's point of view. *Focus on Exceptional Children, 17,* 1-16.

Faraone, S.U., Biederman, J., Lehman, B.K. & Keenan, K. (1993). Evidence for the independent familial transmission of attention deficit hyperactivity disorder and learning disabilities: Results from a family genetic study. *American Journal of Psychiatry, 150*, 891-895.

Fergusson, D.M. & Horwood, L.J. (1992). Attention deficit and reading achievement. *Journal of Child Psychology and Psychiatry, 33*(2), 375-385.

Forness, S.R., Kavale, K.A., Blum, I.M. & Lloyd, J.W. (1997). Mega-analysis of meta-analysis: What works in special education and related services. *Teaching Exceptional Children, 29*(6), 4-9.

Freiberg, K.C. (1992). *Human development*. Boston: Jones and Bartlett.

Friedman, R.J. & Doyal, G.T. (1992). *Management of children and adolescents with attention deficit-hyperactivity disorder*. Austin, TX: Pro-Ed.

Frith, U. (1991). *Autism and Asperger Syndrome*. Cambridge: Cambridge University Press.

Fuchs, D., Fuchs, L.S., Fernstrom, P. & Hohn, M. (1991). Towards a responsible reintegration of behaviorally disordered students. *Behavioral Disorders*, 16(2), 133-147.

Fuller, J., Miller, J. & Lesh, B. (1989). *A resource guide for Oregon educators on developing student responsibility*. Salem, OR: Oregon Department of Education.

Gettinger, M. (1986). Issues and trends in academic engaged time of students. *Special Services in the School, 2*(4), 1-17.

Gillberg, C. & Coleman, M. (1992). *The biology of the autistic syndromes*. London: MacKeith.

Gilbert, P. (1996). *The A-Z reference book of syndromes and inherited disorders* (2nd Ed.). London: Chapman & Hall.

Glasser, W. (1969). *Schools without failure*. New York: Harper & Row.

Glasser, W. (1977). 10 Steps to good discipline. *Today's Education, 66*(4), 61-63.

Glasser, W. (1993). *The quality school teacher*. New York: Harper Collins.

Glasser, W. (1998). *The quality school-managing students without coercion*. New York: Harper Perennial.

Goldstein, S. (Ed.). (1995). *Attention deficit hyperactivity disorder.* New York: John Wiley & Sons.

Goldstein, S. (1995). *Understanding and managing children's' classroom behaviour*, New York: John Wiley & Sons.

Gordon, T. (1970). *Parent effectiveness training.* New York: Plume.

Gordon, T. (1974). *Teacher effectiveness training.* New York: Peter H. Wyden.

Gordon, T. (1991). *Teaching children self-discipline at home and at school.* Sydney: Random House.

Grainger, J. (1997). *Children's' behaviour, attention and reading problems.* Melbourne: ACER.

Hall, C.S. & Linszay, G. (1970). *Theories of personality.* (2nd Ed.), New York: John Wiley & Sons.

Hempenstall, K. (1996). The gulf between educational research and policy. *Behaviour Change, 13,* 33-46.

Hinshaw, S.P. (1992). Externalizing behaviour problems and academic achievement in childhood and adolescence: Causal relationships and underlying mechanisms. *Psychological Bulletin, 111,* 127-155.

Hubbard, J.A. & Newcomb, A.F. (1991). Initial dyadic peer interaction of Attention Deficit-Hyperactivity Disorder and normal boys. *Journal of Abnormal Child Psychology, 19*(2), 179-195.

Hudson, A. (1997). Classroom instruction for children with ADHD. *Australian Journal of Early Childhood, 22*(4), 24-28.

Hynd, G.W., Hern, K.L., Voeller, K.K. & Marshall, R.M. (1991). Neurobiological basis of attention deficit hyperactivity disorder (ADHD). *School Psychology Review, 20*(2), 174-186.

Jarman, F.C. (1996). Current approaches to the management of Attention-Deficit Hyperactivity Disorder. *The Australian Educational and Developmental Psychologist, 13,* 46-55.

Jessor, R. & Jessor S. (1977). *Problem behaviour and psychosocial development: A longitudinal study of youth.* New York: Academic Press.

Jones, F.H. (1987a). *Positive classroom discipline.* New York: McGraw-Hill.

Jones, F.H. (1987b). *Positive classroom instruction.* New York: Mc Graw-Hill.

Jordan, R. & Powell, S. (1995). *Understanding and teaching children with autism.* Chichester: John Wiley.

Kauffman, J. (1985). *Characteristics of children's behavior disorders* (3rd Ed.), Columbus, OH, Charles E. Merrill.

Kohlberg, L. (1969). Stage and sequence: The cognitive–developmental approach to socialization. In D.A. Goslin (Ed.), *Handbook of socialization theory and research* (pp.347-480). Chicago: Rand McNally.

Kohlberg, L. (1976). Moral stages and moralization: The cognitive-developmental point of view. In T. Lickona (Ed.), *Moral development and behaviour: Theory, research and social issues* (pp.31-53). New York: Holt.

Kohlberg, L. (1978). Revisions in the theory and practice of moral development. In W. Damon (Ed.), *New directions for child development* (No. 2, pp.83-87). San Francisco: Jossey-Bass.

Konza, D.M. (1999). An effective teaching model based on classroom observations of students with Attention Deficit Hyperactivity Disorder. Unpublished doctoral thesis, University of Wollongong.

Kounin, J. (1970). *Discipline and group management in classrooms.* New York: Holt, Rinehart & Wilson.

Kuhne, M., Schachar, R. & Tannock, R. (1997). Impact of comorbid oppositional or conduct problems on ADHD. *Journal of the American Academy of Child and Adolescent Psychiatry,* 40(12), 568-581.

Landau, S. & Milich, R. (1988). Social communication patterns of attention deficit disordered boys. *Journal of Abnormal Child Psychology,* 16(1), 69-81.

Landrum, M.S. & Landrum, T.J. (1995). Perceived problem behaviour in intellectually gifted children. *Research Briefs,* 10, 34-43.

Laufer, M. & Denhoff, E. (1957). Hyperkinetic behavior syndrome in children. *Journal of Pediatrics,* 50, 463-474.

Lazarus, R. & Folkman, S. (1984). *Stress appraisal and coping.* New York: Springer.

Lerner, J.W., Lowenthal, B. & Lerner, S.R. (1995). *Attention deficit disorders.* Pacific Grove, CA: Brooks/Cole Pub Co.

Levy, F., Hay, D. & McLaughlin, M. (1996). Twin and sibling differences in parental reports of ADHD, speech, reading and behaviour problems. *Journal of Child Psychiatry and Psychology, 37*(5), 569-578.

Levy, F., Hay, D. & McStephen, M. (1997). *Attention Deficit Hyperactivity Disorder: a category or a continuum? Genetic analysis of a large scale twin study.* Paper presented at the Conference of the NSW Institute of Educational Research, University of New South Wales.

Mathes, P. & Fuchs, L.S. (1994). The efficacy of peer tutoring in reading for students with mild disabilities: A best evidence synthesis. *School Psychology Review, 23*(1), 59-80.

McCarty, H. & Chalmers, L. (1997). Bibliotherapy: Intervention and prevention. *Teaching Exceptional Children, 29*(6), 12-13; 16-17.

McDonnell, J., Thorsen, N., McQuivey, C. & Kiefer-O'Donnell, R. (1996). *The academic engaged time of students with low incidence disabilities in general education classes.* (Research 143): American Educational Research Association.

Ottord, D., Boyle, M. & Racene, Y. (1989). Ontario Child Health Study: Correlates of disorder. *Journal of the American Academy of Child and Adolescent Psychiatry, 28*, 856-861.

Palmer, J. & Neal, P. (1994). *The handbook of environmental education.* London: Routledge.

Pardeck, J.T. & Markward, M. (1994). Bibliotherapy: Using books to help children deal with problems. *Early Child Development and Care, 106,* 75-90.

Parker, H.C. (1992). *The ADD hyperactivity handbook for schools.* Plantation, FL: Impact.

Parker. W.D. & Adkins, K.K. (1995). Perfectionism and the gifted. *Roeper Review*, February/March, 173-176.

Patterson, G.R. (1982). Coercive family process. Eugene, OR: Castalia Press.

Pelham, W.E., Greenslade, K.E., Vodde-Hamilton, M., Murphy, D.A., Greenstein, J.J., Gnagy, E.M., Guthrie, K.L. & Dahl, R.E. (1990). Relative efficacy of long acting stimulants on children with attention deficit-hyperactivity disorder: A comparison of standard methylphenidate, sustained release methylphenidate, sustained release of dextroamphetamine and pemoline. *Pediatrics, 86,* 226-237.

Pelligrini, A.D. & Horvat, M. (1995). A developmental contextualist critique of attention deficit hyperactivity disorder. *Educational Researcher, 24*(1), 13-19.

Piaget, J. (1950). *The psychology of intelligence.* New York: International Universities Press.

Piaget, J. (1952). *The origins of intelligence in children.* New York: International Universities Press. (Original work published 1936.)

Piaget, J. (1985). *The equilibration of cognitive structures: The central problem of intellectual development.* Chicago: University of Chicago Press.

Pisarchick, S.E. (1989). *The importance of time management skills for the child or adolescent with learning disabilities.* Paper presented at the International Conference of the Association for Children and Adults with Learning Disabilities, Miami, FL.

Prior, M. (1996). Implications of ADHD for learning. *The Australian Educational and Developmental Psychologist, 13,* 24-28.

Purvis, J.R., Jones, C.H. & Authement, C. (1992). Attention deficit hyperactivity disorder: Strategies for the classroom. *B.C. Journal of Special Education, 16*(2), 112-119.

Redl, F. (1972). *When we deal with children: Selected writings.* New York: Free Press.

Reid, R., Maag, J.W. & Vasa, S.F. (1993). Attention deficit hyperactivity disorder as a disability category: A critique. *Exceptional Children, 60*(3), 198-214.

Rhode, G., Jenson, W.R. & Reavis, H.K. (1992). *The tough kid book: Practical classroom management strategies.* Longmont, CO: Sopris West.

Richard, G. (1997). *The source for autism.* East Moline, IL: LinguiSystems, Inc.

Rogers, W. (1989). *Making a discipline plan: Developing classroom management skills.* Melbourne: Nelson.

Rogers, W. (1993). *The language of discipline: A practical approach to effective classroom management.* Plymouth, UK: Northcote House.

Rogers, W. (1994). *Behaviour recovery.* Melbourne: ACER.

Rogers, W. (1995). *Behaviour management.* Gosford, NSW: Ashton Scholastic.

Rogers, W. (1998). *'You know the fair rule' and much more: Strategies for making the hard job of discipline and behaviour management in school easier*. Melbourne: A.C.E.R.

Rosenshine, B. & Stevens, R. (1986). Teaching functions. In M. C. Wittrock (Ed.), *Handbook of research on teaching* (3rd ed., pp.376-391). New York: Macmillan.

Ruddell, B.R. (1995). Those influential literacy teachers: Meaning negotiators and motivation builders. *The Reading Teacher, 48,* 454-463.

Rutter, M., Maughan, B., Mortimore, P. & Ouston, J. (1979). *Fifteen thousand hours*. London: Open Books.

Salkovskis, P.M. (1996). *Frontiers of cognitive therapy*. New York: Guildford Press.

Sanson, A.V., Pedlow, R., Cann, W., Prior, M. & Oberklaid, F. (1996). Shyness ratings: Stability and correlates in early childhood. *International Journal of Behavioural Development, 19,* 704-724.

Sarafino, E.P. (1998). *Health psychology*. New York: John Wiley.

Satterfield, J.J., Hoppe, C.M. & Schell, A.M. (1982). A prospective study of delinquency in 110 adolescent boys with attention deficit disorder and 88 normal adolescent boys. *American Journal of Psychiatry, 139,* 795-798.

Scherer, M., Gersch, I. & Fry, L. (1990). *Meeting disruptive behaviour: Assessment, intervention and partnership*. London: Macmillan.

Scruggs, T.E. & Mastropieri, M.A. (1992). Effective mainstreaming strategies for mildly handicapped students. *Elementary School Journal, 92*(3), 389-409.

Selye, R. (1985). History and present status of the stress concept. In A. Monat & R. Lazarus (Eds.), *Stress and coping*. 2nd Ed. New York: Colombia Press.

Shaywitz, B.A. & Shaywitz, S.E. (1991). Comorbidity: A critical issue in attention deficit disorder. *Journal of Child Neurology, 6*(supplement), S13-18.

Shaywitz, B.A., Fletcher, J.M. & Shaywitz, S.E. (Eds.), (1992). *Interrelationships between reading disability and attention deficit hyperactivity disorder*. Baltimore: York Press, Inc.

Skinner, B.F. (1989). *Recent issues in the analysis of behaviour*. Colombus, OH: Merrill.

Silverman, L.K. (1994). The moral sensitivity of gifted children and the evolution of society. *Roeper Review*, 17(2), 110-116.

Simonoff, E., Pickles, A., Meyer, J., Silberg, J. & Maes, H. (1998). Genetic and environmental influences on subtypes of conduct disorder behaviour in boys. *Journal of Abnormal Psychology*, 26(6), 495-509.

Sridhar, D. & Vaughn, S. (2000). Bibliotherapy for all: Enhancing reading comprehension, self-concept and behavior. *Teaching Exceptional Children*, 33(2), 74-82.

Steiner, H., Dunne, J., Ayres, W., Arnold, V., Benedek, E., Benson, S., Bernstein, G., Bernet, W., Bukstein, O., Kinlan, J., Leonard, H. & McClellan, J. (1997). Practice parameters for the assessment and treatment of children and adolescents with conduct disorder. *Journal of the American Academy of Child and Adolescent Psychiatry*, 36(10), 1225-1237.

Still, G.F. (1902). Some abnormal psychical conditions in children. *Lancet*, *1*, 1008-1012.

Szatmari, P., Boyle, M. & Offord, D.R. (1989). ADHD and conduct disorder: Degree of diagnostic overlap and differences among correlates. *Journal of the American Academy of Child and Adolescent Psychiatry*, 28, 865-872.

Tauber, R.T. (1995). *Classroom management: Theory and practice* (2nd Ed.), Orlando, FL: Holt, Rinehart & Winston.

Thurlow, M.L., Ysseldyke, J.E. & Wotruba, J.W. (1988). *A case study analysis of factors related to effective student-teacher ratios*. (Instructional Alternatives Project): University of Minnesota.

Trautman, R.C., Giddan, J.J. & Jurs, S.G. (1990). Language risk factor in emotionally disturbed children within a school and day treatment program. *Journal of Childhood Communication Disorders*, 13, 123-133.

Trevarthen, C., Aitken, K., Papoudi, D. & Roberts, J. (1996). *Children with autism: Diagnosis and interventions to meet their needs*. London: Jessica Kingsley Publishers.

von Bertalanffy, L. (1968). *General systems theory: Foundations, developments, applications*. London: Allen Lane The Penguin Press.

Wallace, G. & McLaughlin, J.A. (1988). *Learning disabilities: Concepts and characteristics*, 3rd Ed. Columbus, OH: Merrill.

Walker, J.E. & Shea, T.M. (1991). *Behaviour management*. New York: Merrill.

Werner, H. & Strauss, A. (1941). Pathology of the figure-background relation in the child. *Journal of Abnormal and Social Psychology, 36*, 234-248.

Westwood, P. (1993). Mixed ability teaching: Issues of personalization, inclusivity and effective instruction. *Australian Journal of Remedial Education, 25*(2), 22-26.

Wheldall, K. & Carter, M. (1996). Reconstructing behaviour analysis in education: A revised behavioural interactionist perspective for special education. *Educational Psychology, 16*(2), 121-140.

Whitman, T.L., Scherzinger, M.L. & Sommer, K.S. (1991). Cognitive instruction and mental retardation. In P. Kendall (Ed.), *Child and adolescent therapy: Cognitive-behavioral procedures*. New York: Guildford.

Wing, L. (1996). *The autistic spectrum*. London: Constable.

Wing, L. & Gould, J. (1979). Severe impairments of social interaction and associated abnormalities in children: epidemiology and classification, *Journal of Autisn and Childhood Schizophrenia, 9*, 11-29.

Wragg, J. (1989). *Talk sense to yourself*. Melbourne: ACER.

Yates, G.R. (1988). Classroom research into effective teaching. *Australian Journal of Remedial Education, 20*(1), 4-9.

Yehle, A.K. & Wambold, C. (1998). An ADHD success story: Strategies for teachers and students. *Teaching Exceptional Children, 30*(6), 8-13.

Young-Loveridge, J. (1997). A personal perspective on challenging behaviour: ADHD? *Australian Journal of Early Childhood, 22*(4), 1-6.

Zametkin, A.J. & Rapoport, J.L. (1987). Neurobiology of attention deficit disorder with hyperactivity: Where have we come in 50 years? *American Academy of Child and Adolescent Psychiatry, 26*, 676-686.

Zentall, S.S. (1993). Research on the educational implications of attention deficit hyperactivity disorder. *Exceptional Children, 60*(2), 143-153.